The Best Days
of Our Lives

The Best Days of Our Lives

School Life in Post-War Britain

Simon Webb

First published 2013

The History Press
The Mill, Brimscombe Port
Stroud, Gloucestershire, GL5 2QG
www.thehistorypress.co.uk

British Library Cataloguing in Publication Data.
A catalogue record for this book is available from the British Library.

ISBN 978 0 7524 8637 6

Typesetting and origination by The History Press
Printed in Great Britain

Contents

Acknowledgements

Many thanks go to those who contributed their memories of school life during the 1940s and 1950s: Keith J. Ballard, Peter A. Barker, Ellen T. Cade, Dorothy Dobson, Lilian O. Drake, Sheila Fawcett, Ronald G. Feeney, John B. Fleming, Lorna Gavin, James R. Harker, Brenda Jacobs, Catherine E. Kingsley, Margaret L. Jones, Caroline T. Maxted, Patrick J. McGuire, Glynn Mitchell, Mary Olive, Gregory Parker, Joyce L. Pettitt, Paul M. Richardson, Philip F.A. Robertson, James H. Schneider, Harry R. Smith, Conrad Summerfield, David P. Taylor, Janet L. Thompson, Victor C. Webb and Josephine A. Wilson. Without their help, it would not have been possible to write this book.

Introduction

This is an account of children's experiences of school life in Britain during the fifteen years following the Second World War. During that time, education in this country was dominated by the 11-plus examination which divided children at state schools into those who went to grammar schools at the age of eleven and the great majority who did not. The experience of the 11-plus marked every child during this period, except for those at independent schools.

At least three quarters of children at school during the post-war years 'failed' the 11-plus and ended up attending secondary modern schools. However, the very word 'failed' is an inappropriate one to use in this context. When the 11-plus was first devised nobody was thinking of it in terms of an examination which could be passed or failed. Its aim was to simply allocate children to the type of secondary school best suited to their needs and abilities. Despite the huge impact which it had at the time, it should be borne in mind that the 11-plus was only around for twenty years or so; starting at the end of the Second World War and coming to an end in most of the country in the mid-1960s.

The history of this 75 per cent or more of children who were neither privately educated nor attended grammar schools has often been neglected and sometimes entirely overlooked. Fictional accounts of childhood during this time, from the *Famous Five* stories of Enid Blyton and C.S. Lewis's *Chronicles of Narnia* to the *St Trinian's* films, show a world where independent, fee-paying schools are the norm. Real life reminiscences of school in the 1940s and '50s seem to focus upon the lives of children at grammar and private schools, rather than exploring life at ordinary primary schools and secondary moderns. Through the first-hand testimonies of those who were at school from 1945 to 1960, this book looks at how life was at secondary moderns, as well as grammar schools.

Before the Second World War the overwhelming majority of children left school at fourteen with no qualifications at all. Surprisingly, this situation continued up to 1960, at which time around 80 per cent of secondary school pupils were still leaving school without sitting any examinations and consequently leaving with no qualifications. This meant that most children leaving school could not even think of being able to attend university.

The 11-plus was so important to school children in the post-war years that this book looks in some detail at the real reasons why so many of them ended up in secondary modern schools, leaving school at fifteen with nothing much to show for their years of education. Many older people still feel bitter about their apparent 'failure', but, as we shall see, there was good deal more to success or failure in the 11-plus than met the eye.

At the end of this book is a list of further reading for those interested in finding out more about school life in the post-war years.

Simon Webb, 2013

All Change – The 1944 'Butler Act'

Any account of British schools in the years following the Second World War must begin with the 1944 Education Act, commonly called the Butler Act, which began the selective education system which existed in this country until the mid-1960s. The Butler Act (named after a Conservative politician of the time, Robert Austen Butler – known affectionately as 'Rab') sought to sweep away the elementary schools attended by 90 per cent of schoolchildren and replace them with a system which guaranteed free secondary education to everybody up to the age of fifteen.

As the Second World War drew to a close, it was becoming clear to most people in Britain that life in their country would be very different after the war from the way it was before. A young, working-class man summed it up like this:

> There's a story about Lord Curzon during the First World War. Apparently, he was watching a bunch of Tommies stripped to the waist and washing in a stream. He's supposed to have said, 'I never knew that the lower classes had such white skins'. You can just about believe that an aristocrat in the 1914-1918 war was like that; it's impossible to imagine it in 1940. I remember being a fire watcher during the Blitz, on the roof of a building in the city, passing information to the ARP. We worked in pairs and I was teamed up sometimes with this Right Honourable. If it wasn't for the war we would never have even met, but as we got talking during the night watch and both found that we weren't so very different from each other. Both dead keen on

girls, drinking and the horses. It was obvious that though we spoke differently, we had a lot in common. It seemed to me as the war ended that Britain wasn't going to be divided up into officers and 'other ranks' so much in the future. After all, people were calling it a 'war for democracy'. (Victor C. Webb)

The Second World War was a great leveller in a way that the First World War had not been. For one thing, there was the shared terror of the German air raids, which threatened everybody alike, regardless of class or social background. Professional men, like solicitors and accountants, huddled in air-raid shelters at night alongside lorry drivers and Dockers. At the same time, the hundreds of thousands of city children evacuated to the countryside helped bring a greater understanding between the rural and urban communities of Britain. The war in general and the Blitz in particular drew everybody together and showed them what they had in common, as opposed to how they differed from each other.

British society, before the outbreak of war in 1939, had been divided by class and that division began with and was to a large extent defined by education and schooling.

Before I started school, I was looked after by a nanny, who was an extremely snobby woman. I was taken to the park, but Nanny kept a sharp eye on me and called me over at once if it looked as though the wrong sort of children were arriving at the sandpit. When I started school, this separation from others became even more pronounced. I was at a prep school in West London, and there simply wasn't any opportunity to meet boys outside my school and home circle. (James R. Harker)

In the 1940s, by the age of twelve, most children's paths in life were practically pre-ordained. If you knew what sort of school a child attended at that age, you would have a pretty good idea what sort of life they were going to have and what sort of job they would be doing as an adult. By the age of fifteen, these probabilities had become certainties; the child's future was essentially set in stone. To see why this should have been, it will be necessary to examine the sort of educational system which was operating in this country during the final years of the Second World War.

Today, we are so used to children from all kinds of backgrounds sitting examinations and leaving school with various qualifications that it comes as something of a shock to learn that until 1945, 90 per cent of children in Britain left school at the age of fourteen with no qualifications of any kind. To gain the School Certificate, the equivalent of present-day GCSEs, it was necessary to stay at school until the age of sixteen. Since the great majority of children attended elementary schools, which catered only for teenagers up to the age of fourteen, gaining the School Certificate simply wasn't possible for most pupils.

> I don't even remember having the chance to sit the scholarship for a high school. I suppose I must have been told about it, but I was at an elementary school in the last years of the war, and we all left at the age of fourteen, which was the practice back then. It would have seemed strange to do anything other than leave at fourteen. I didn't even know what the School Certificate was until I was asked if I had it in later years when I was applying for a job. You had to stay on to the age of sixteen to get the School Certificate, and I certainly didn't know anybody who spent that long at school. Straight away, there were a lot of jobs that you couldn't really get without having the School Certificate. If you wanted to work in an office, they wanted the School Certificate because it showed that you could read and write well, amongst other things. (Margaret L. Jones)

Entering further education without the School Certificate was all but impossible, and it was also very hard to get anything other than manual work without it. Even an ordinary clerical job could prove hard to come by without this vital piece of paper – the proof that one had been educated beyond the absolute bare minimum level. The only way to continue education to the age of sixteen was through either an independent school or a grammar school. The grammar schools were also fee paying, although a quarter of their places were set aside for scholarship pupils. In theory, this meant that any child could sit the entrance exam at eleven and gain a free place; in practice, many of these places were monopolised by middle-class families who couldn't quite afford the fees. Very few went to working-class children whose parents were manual workers. Even when a bright working-class child was offered the opportunity for a place at a grammar school, there could be other problems:

My teacher wanted me to sit the exam and try for a scholarship at the grammar school when I was eleven, but my parents wouldn't hear of it. It was bad enough for them that it would be another three years until I could start earning, never mind waiting until I was sixteen or eighteen. Besides, what was the point in a girl staying on at school like that? The teacher even came round to the house to talk to them, but it was no good. So I stayed on at the elementary school and left when I was fourteen and went to work in the same factory as all my friends. (Janet L. Thompson)

I don't think people today can have any idea of how important it was for children to start earning as soon as possible. That extra wage made all the difference. My mother was counting the days until I left school, knowing how much easier is would make things for the whole family. Once I started, I did what my older brother did, just handed over my wage packet to her. She then gave us back some pocket money, enough to go out on Saturday night. By the time I actually got my first wages, she had already pledged herself in credit at the shops on the strength of my first money. I can tell you, it would have been a right problem for her if I'd turned round and told her that I wanted to stop on at school for another few years. (Gregory Parker)

For other families, the loss of a wage was not the only financial consideration which prevented the child from taking up an offered place at a grammar school. One of the great distinguishing marks of the grammar school or private school pupil was that they wore uniforms. Children at elementary schools wore whatever their parents felt like dressing them in. Starting grammar school, though, meant a trip to an expensive shop for coats, blazers, shirts, ties, trousers, gymslips, caps, hats, games kit, shoes and so on. For many working families, it was simply not possible to find the money for such things. It was enough of a struggle to put food on the table each day without having to kit a child out in this way – this was a time when most children had just one pair of shoes and one coat. Grants were sometimes available, but getting one could be a chancy business.

I passed the scholarship for the grammar school, but when my mother and father found out how much it would cost for me to go there, the whole thing fell through. They had already been fretting about how they would find the money for the bus fare each day; the grammar school was six or seven miles away. When they received the uniform list and totted it all up, that was it. I was an only child and that meant, for some reason, that they weren't entitled to a grant for the uniform. I don't recall being much bothered about it to be honest. It meant that I would be staying at the elementary school with all my mates. (Gregory Parker)

I passed the scholarship exam and got a place at grammar school. At first it all nearly went wrong from the first, because my parents were told that they weren't entitled to a grant for the uniform. This would have sounded the death knell for any chance of me going to the grammar – they couldn't possibly have afforded to kit me out from their own money. It turned out that they had made a mistake in their application. It was like The Family at One End Street. My father had somehow ticked a box saying that I was an only child, rather than one of five. Once that had been sorted out, we got the grant. There were still a lot of other expenses that weren't covered by the uniform grant; things to do with sports and days out. Sometimes I had to miss out on school trips because we couldn't afford to contribute. In some ways, I felt like a charity child, at least compared with those whose parents were paying fees, which was most of them. (Mary Olive)

The elementary schools, which almost all children attended, had their roots in the Victorian era and had originally been set up to educate children whose only prospect was to end up working on farms or in factories. They were known in the nineteenth century as 'industrial schools' and aimed to provide no more than basic instruction in literacy and numeracy. By the time children left elementary school, they were expected to be able to read a paragraph from a newspaper, work out the change from a shopping trip and take down simple dictation; that was it, little or nothing in the way of history, geography, science or literature. In many ways, these schools had hardly changed from the late nineteenth century up to the outbreak of war in 1939.

The sort of things we learned when we were twelve or thirteen weren't much different from what we'd been doing when we were nine.

Nothing special happened at eleven, not in the way that kids now move up to secondary school. It was more or less the same all the way through till we left at fourteen. I suppose the best way of looking at it is that our school life in the elementary was just like being at a big junior school from five to fourteen. (Gregory Parker)

The three Rs and, of course, a lot of PE and practical stuff, that was about it. Housework for the girls, only they called it 'Mothercraft', and woodwork for the boys. It was like everybody, all the teachers I mean, had already decided that there wasn't much point in doing a lot with us. They knew we were only going to work with our hands and we wouldn't need a lot of book-learning for that. In most cases they were probably right, but it would have been nice to have had the chance to try other stuff. We couldn't all have been so thick that we would only be fit to operate a tractor on the farm or bit of machinery in a factory! (Sheila Fawcett)

Such schools had long outlived their day, and even before the Second World War it was obvious that the state school system needed to be overhauled. The desire to change things and extend secondary education to all children did not come from those whose children were attending the elementary schools. Nor did it come from the pupils themselves; most working-class children couldn't wait to leave school and start working, and their parents usually felt the same way.

The introduction of compulsory schooling in the late nineteenth century had been very unpopular with many working-class families, depriving them as it did of another wage earner. In the 1880s, prosecutions of parents for not sending their children to school were more common than any other offence in Britain, apart from drunkenness. This reluctance to have a child 'wasting' time in school when he could be earning a wage lingered on well into the 1940s and '50s. The frantic desire to leave school at the earliest opportunity was worrying to local authorities, and it was the subject of a government enquiry in the mid-1950s. It was found that working-class pupils not only left the newly established secondary moderns at fifteen, but that exactly the same thing was going on in the grammar schools, with around a quarter of working-class pupils attending them also leaving at fifteen, before they had a chance to sit any examinations.

I passed my 11-plus and went to the grammar school. I didn't much like it though. A lot of what they were doing there didn't seem to have much to do with my life, my interests. I suppose, to be fair, I might have felt the same way if I'd gone to the secondary modern, but I couldn't wait to leave. This was in 1953, just after they had scrapped the School Certificate and brought in GCEs. There was some talk of me stopping on and taking the GCE, but I didn't want to spend another year there, I wanted to get a job. I think my parents were pleased, although if I'd wanted to stay on, they would have let me. They were glad to have another wage coming in when I left school. (Glynn Mitchell)

To some extent it is possible to sympathise with the families who felt this way. Teenagers are notoriously expensive to clothe and feed, and money was desperately tight in many homes. The moment that a fourteen-year-old began bringing home a wage could make the difference between being at the point of near starvation and just scraping by.

During the war, the situation in Britain was that many, perhaps most, parents and children saw the years spent in the elementary school as an irrelevant interlude before the age of fourteen was reached and the child was able to get a job. The realisation that this was not a satisfactory state of affairs and the desire to alter the system mainly came from educated men and women, those who had been to university themselves, and their ideas were widely resented by the very people whom they were trying to help.

I hated being stuck at school, 'specially once I was twelve or thirteen. I was in an elementary school, having to spend all day with kids as young as five. Our school worked on the monitor system, where older pupils taught the younger ones. Here I was, couldn't wait to join my Dad in the shipyard in a few months and until then being made to help teach the alphabet to a load of infants. Most of the other boys in the school felt the same way. It seemed so unfair. We were big enough to do a days work and yet we were being made to stay with children all day. I didn't know anybody at our school who went on to secondary school. I suppose I'd heard that you could sit for a scholarship to a grammar school, but really, I would have refused point-blank if anybody had suggested anything of the sort. I wanted to be out in the world earning a wage. As for what my Dad would have said about me spending another three or four years at school, well, he wouldn't have heard of it. We needed another wage coming in and as soon as possible. (Paul M. Richardson)

As we shall see, this attitude persisted among many families until well after the introduction of free secondary education for all children; with the majority leaving at the first opportunity at the age of fifteen, rather than staying on for another year. The tendency to view school as some sort of irritating institution was still around as late as the early 1970s, when the school leaving age was officially raised to sixteen.

> I was at a secondary modern in 1951 and was just marking time till I was fifteen and could leave and go to work. Although I'd failed my 11-plus, I wasn't too bad at schoolwork, and one day the head sent for me. He said that I might be able to transfer to a grammar school if I sat another exam. This was what came to be known as the 13-plus, it was another chance for those who'd failed their 11-plus. He talked about going to the grammar school, maybe entering the sixth form there and perhaps even going to university. I listened politely, saying 'Yes, sir' and 'No, sir' in all the right places. I didn't even tell my parents about it, I was that horrified at the thought of staying at school for longer than I had to. As for switching schools and leaving all my mates, well it just wasn't going to happen. He wrote to my parents, but they didn't care. My father had managed alright without much of an education, and so I stayed on at the secondary modern and left at fifteen like everybody else. (Lorna Gavin)

We are so used to regarding the key ages in a young person's life as being eleven, sixteen and eighteen, that it comes as something of a shock to realise that until the 1940s, boys of fourteen were regarded generally as grown men; capable of putting in a full day's work at a man's job.

> I was furious when I realised that the new law would mean I had to stay on at school for another year. It was announced in the spring of 1947 and I would have turned fourteen in the October. I felt that I had been cheated out of becoming an adult. My parents were none too

pleased about it either. Things were a bit of a struggle and they had been counting on having another wage coming in in the autumn.

There didn't seem to be any sense in making us stay on at school for longer. We wanted the jobs, the employers wanted to have us, and now we were being told that we would have to wait another year until we could leave. It wasn't as though that year would make any difference to us. We mostly knew what we would be doing. (Sheila Fawcett)

It was attitudes such as these, among both parents and children, which had prevented any progress being made with the plan to extend secondary education to all children in Britain. Nobody really wanted it; not the parents, the children, the teachers, nor the local authorities. The existing system had worked well enough for decades and to change it would mean a great deal of expense and upheaval. It is worth noting that it was not only children in elementary schools who could not see the point of remaining at school and were keen to get out into the 'real world'. Here are two grammar school pupils' points of view:

I was at a grammar school from 1941 until 1946. I didn't want to stay on for the sixth form. I was a scholarship boy, and I have to say that most of what we were being taught didn't seem to have any sort of connection with the real world. What really brought it home to me was the business of Latin pronunciation. We followed what was known as the 'New Pronunciation'. About fifty years earlier, some people had worked out that the Romans actually pronounced 'V' as 'W' and that 'C' was always hard, like 'K'. This meant that we were supposed to call *Cicero*, 'Kickero'. Common Latin expressions like *vice versa* were also pronounced in the new way, we would learn to say 'wicky worser', rather than *vice versa*. Anyway, there were furious debates about this, with half the class preferring the old-style pronunciation and others being very partisan for the new way. Even the teachers had strong views on the matter. This was all going on in 1945, when I was fifteen. Here we were, in the year that Belsen was on the newsreels and the atom bomb dropped on Japan and I was spending my days with people who were more bothered about how to pronounce the name of some statesman who had been dead for two thousand years. There was something utterly unreal about it. (David P. Taylor)

> I think I can safely say that since I left school in 1949, I have never
> once found occasion to say, 'Hand me the spear, O my brother' in Latin.
> As for the vocative case, I have never been able to fathom why anybody
> thought that it would be a good use of a twelve-year-old's time to teach
> her that *mensa* meant 'O table'. I mean, I have never been in the habit
> of addressing my table in English, never mind Latin. (Mary Olive)

So far we have looked mainly at the views of working-class children
who, after the war, would almost invariably end up in the new secondary
modern schools. The perspective from those whose parents were paying
to have them educated was rather different. Take the pupils above for
instance, who couldn't imagine why they were being forced to learn Latin,
and what's more to pronounce the language in a particular way. What
possible relevance did Latin pronunciation have in a world just emerging
from the most terrible war the world had ever known? Surprisingly
enough, it was of paramount importance for the future prospects of
those children whose parents were hoping that they would be able to
attend Oxford or Cambridge Universities. A boy who attended a private
preparatory school in the late 1940s explains:

> By the time I was eleven, I was studying Latin and Greek to a pretty
> high standard. I remember telling my father one day that I couldn't
> see the point in it; I wasn't ever going to meet any Romans or ancient
> Greeks, so why spend all that time learning their languages? I asked
> why I couldn't learn German or French instead. His answer was short
> and to the point. 'You want to get to Oxford, don't you?' I mumbled
> something like, 'I suppose so,' and that was that. I still didn't twig, but
> one didn't really argue with my father. If he said I wanted to get to
> Oxford, then I supposed that I must do! It wasn't until I was in the sixth
> that I found out about Responsions and then it all made sense and I
> was glad that I had spent all that time swotting up on dead languages.
> (James R. Harker)

There is regular discussion these days in the newspapers about the
proportion of state school pupils getting into top universities such as
Oxford, but despite this the situation between the end of the Second
World War and 1960 was breathtakingly different. At least today, every
child at a state school has a theoretical possibility of attending Oxford

or Cambridge. Before 1960, the chances of over three quarters of state school pupils of getting a place at Oxbridge were, quite literally, zero. The reason for this was the entrance examinations in operation at both universities.

Entry to both Oxford and Cambridge Universities meant having to pass examinations in Latin, Greek and mathematics. At Oxford this process was called the 'Responsions'. Obviously, only those at private schools or grammar schools would be studying these dead languages, without which there was no possibility of getting to Oxbridge. For fifteen years after the end of the Second World War, this remained the case; effectively barring the 75 per cent or so of pupils attending secondary modern schools from these universities. Until 1960, only those with a good working knowledge of Latin and Greek could even hope to get into Oxford.

When I went up to Cambridge in 1954, it was still very much a case of the Old Boys' Network. My father had been there and his father had also been there. They both went to the same college, which was the one I was applying for. I had some A levels, although they weren't brilliant. The important thing though was that I was pretty good at Latin, Greek and Algebra. I sailed through the entrance exam, my father having paid some penniless student to coach me during the holidays. And that was it; I was in. Whatever strings could be pulled in the background, and I'm sure my father was just the man to do this, it was no good if one didn't have enough Latin and Greek to get through the entrance exam. That was crucial and I have no doubt that there were boys at ordinary state grammar schools who were much brighter than me but who didn't stand a chance of getting into Cambridge because they didn't have Latin. (Conrad Summerfield)

The 1944 Education Act, or the Butler Act, came about as a result of the wartime government's determination to eradicate poverty, unemployment, ignorance, squalor and disease in the post-war society for which they were already preparing. The tackling of these five 'giant evils', as identified in the 1942 Beveridge Report, was to eventually lead to the foundation of the welfare state. Robert Austen Butler, who was appointed to the post of President of the Board of Education by Prime Minister Winston Churchill in 1941, at the height of the Second World War, was given the responsibility of creating this.

The scheme which Butler championed entailed raising the school leaving age first to fifteen and then sixteen and ensuring that every child in the country should have free access to secondary education. As originally envisaged, this would be a tripartite system of grammar, technical and secondary modern schools. The technical schools never really took off and so what remained were grammar and secondary modern schools.

> Intelligence tests, or IQ tests as they were also known, were a big thing just after the war. I was a teenager at that time and already at secondary school, but I can remember the excitement that was felt about the whole thing. Of course, there were scholarships for school places at grammars, but we understood the 11-plus to be something quite different from an ordinary scholarship exam. As we understood it, these boffins in white coats had come up with a way to measure intelligence, a series of tests that would let them know not only how clever you were, but even how clever you were likely to be in the future. It was supposed to have nothing at all to do with how hard you worked or what school you had gone to. One look at the results of this new test and they would be able to see at a glance how your mind worked. (Mary Olive)

These changes to the educational system were being made with the best of intentions and did actually enable working-class children to go to grammar schools. Grants were made available for uniforms if parents were unable to afford them. One early beneficiary of the new scheme recalls his father's views:

> It always stuck in my father's craw that it was a Tory who arranged things so that working-class kids could have as much chance of going to grammar school as anybody else. I passed the 11-plus in 1947 and went to the local grammar. Before the war, this particular grammar school had been a posh, fee-paying one, and the idea that his son could go there was absolutely astonishing to my father. There had been scholarships available before the war, but only for a small number of children. Now, the whole place was being thrown open for free to any child who could pass the exam. Although he was a staunch socialist, there was no doubt that he admired what Butler had managed to achieve. Making the grammar schools free was an amazing thing

for a Conservative politician to think of. It would be a bit like the government today suddenly privatising Harrow and Eton and insisting that anybody could go there if they simply passed an entrance exam. (Glynn Mitchell)

As a matter of fact, plans were mooted at around the same time for what would have amounted to the privatisation of public schools like Eton. They were encouraged to offer a certain proportion of their places to bright children whose parents could not afford the fees, just as the grammar schools had done in the years before 1939. This scheme came to nothing, as it would have been the local authorities who would have had to subsidise the places, and they felt that the money would be better used to improve schools in their own areas.

In short, from 1945 onwards every child in the country could attend a free secondary school. Raising the school leaving age took a little while to implement and there was considerable opposition to the idea throughout government. The new Education Secretary, Ellen Wilkinson, insisted though and from April 1947 all children were obliged by law to remain at school until the age of fifteen. Increasing the leaving age to sixteen did not become law for another quarter of a century. Although many working-class families resented the raising of the leaving age in this way and regarded the new Act in general as government interference, there were those who saw it as a new opportunity.

My parents were not well educated and we were not well off. Nevertheless, they valued learning and realised that it was a way out of the lifestyle into which they themselves had been channelled. They somehow scraped together the money to get a student to come round and tutor me for a few months before I took the scholarship for grammar school. Heaven knows how they managed to do it, we barely had enough money to buy food and pay the gas bill. It must have worked though, because I passed. They were tremendously proud of me in my new uniform for the grammar school and I think that they basked in a sort of reflected glory as well. Nobody else for miles around had passed the 11-plus and I was the only child getting the bus to the grammar school in the morning from where we lived. They got a grant to pay for the uniform and made sure that I did all the homework that was set. There were very few working-class girls like me at the school and I got the feeling that even the teachers thought it was a mistake inviting the wrong sort of child to the school. Until the 1944 Act, the grammar school had been private. (Ellen T. Cade)

I had never even known any children at the grammar school; it might as well have been on another planet. Then suddenly there was all this talk about it being open to everybody and that it wasn't a matter of having to pay for it any more. It didn't mean a lot to me because I went to the same school that my brother and sister attended. It had been an elementary, but was now supposed to be a primary and secondary modern. Nothing had really changed though. Everybody took it for granted that once you were at the infants there, then that was where you would be spending the rest of the time until you left school. I certainly didn't realise that it would be any different for me. It was though, because I passed the scholarship in 1948 and got a place at the grammar. I learned later that my brother and sister had been a bit put out about it; they thought that I would be getting above myself. We used to make fun of the grammar school children, you see, when we saw them in the street. (Glynn Mitchell)

I remember going to be fitted for my uniform. I would be wearing a school cap, which was then the mark of the grammar schoolboy. I don't think that anything which I subsequently achieved in my life, Oxford and so on, made my mother as proud as seeing her son dressed up in the grammar school uniform, with a cap on his head. It symbolised all that she had never been able to do herself. Although she was sharp enough intellectually, she came from the sort of family where the girls left school at fourteen to go into service or work in a factory or mill. Seeing me in my school cap assured my mother that for her child at least, things would be different. (David P. Taylor)

There is no doubt that the intentions of those who pushed through the reorganisation of schools in this country were well meaning.

When Labour came to power in 1945, the post of Minister of Education went to fifty-four-year-old Ellen Wilkinson. 'Red' Ellen, as she was known, had been one of the organisers of the Jarrow March and was from a working-class family in Manchester. She had been to a high school herself and had then gone on to university. It was her personal background which made her passionately committed to the selective education system which was being put into place in the years immediately following the end of the war.

It is curious to reflect that at this time it was the Labour Party that was strongly in favour of grammar schools. In the modern jargon, they saw them as 'engines of social mobility', which would enable every working-class child to fulfil his or her potential – just as Ellen Wilkinson had been able to do. Her own vision for state schools was plain. Far from the secondary modern schools being dumping grounds for those unable to achieve academically, Wilkinson saw them as exciting and stimulating places, where no child would be left behind. Recalling her own childhood, she said, 'Can't Shakespeare mean more than a scrubbing brush? Can't enough of a foreign language be taught to open windows on the world a bit wider? I learnt French verbs, saying them as I scrubbed floors at home.'

She saw the new schools not as somewhere where youngsters would simply be prepared for a lifetime of drudgery, but as places where there would be laughter in the classroom, self-confidence growing every day, and eager interest instead of bored conformity.

Unfortunately, much of what Ellen Wilkinson hoped to achieve for education in this country came to nothing. Even the simple act of raising the school leaving age from fourteen to fifteen proved a desperate struggle. It may have passed into law with the 1944 Education Act, but many wanted to delay the implementation of this part of the Act indefinitely. She only persuaded the Cabinet to set a date to raise the legal school leaving age in 1947 by threatening to resign.

There was a tremendous spirit of optimism surrounding British education at that time. It went hand-in-hand with the new welfare state which was being put into place. Free secondary education being available to all was a natural accompaniment to free medical treatment for all. The old barriers were coming down, and the Labour government seemed determined to ensure that poverty or class would not prevent anybody from gaining access to either hospital treatment or a decent school for their children in the future.

Those first years after the war were tremendously exciting if you were working class and young. The coal mines had signs outside saying 'Under New Ownership' – our ownership. That's what nationalisation meant to us, that these things belonged to us now rather than the bosses.

It was the same with the hospitals, they were free to everybody and the schools were going the same way. First the grammars and then for a while it looked as though the public schools would all be nationalised as well. We imagined Harrow and Eton having signs outside like the coal mines, saying 'Under New Ownership'. Of course, it was all too good to be true, but there was this great spirit of optimism. (Gregory Parker)

Unfortunately, the best laid plans often go awry in their execution and so it proved with the radical overhaul of the country's education system.

I knew before I sat the 11-plus that my parents intended me to go to the grammar school. They probably wouldn't have been able to afford the fees if it had still been private, but now that it was only a question of passing an examination to get in, they were utterly convinced that I would be going there. Our family were what you might describe as middle class, but had fallen on hard times. My grandfather had been a solicitor, but my father had not wanted to do that. He ran a series of businesses, each less profitable than the one before. We had all the pretensions of an upper middle-class family, but without the finances to support the lifestyle. Nevertheless, my father had friends who were teachers and he persuaded some of these people to coach me for the 11-plus. It wasn't supposed to be possible to do this, but those in the know laughed about this. One of the teachers got hold of the previous years' papers and worked through them with me. I breezed through it without any problem at all. In later years, it has struck me that this was more than a little unfair; that families without the right connections would have been at a distinct disadvantage, but then I suppose it's always been like that. (Keith J. Ballard)

Questions began to be raised about how fair the new school system was to children from poorer backgrounds within a few years or so. One of those who suspected that the 11-plus was cheating young children of an opportunity was Brian Simon, a teacher at Salford Grammar School in the North of England in the late 1940s. Simon watched with interest the academic progress of pupils who transferred to the grammar school from secondary moderns. Some local education authorities offered the possibility of sitting a 'transfer' examination if one had failed the 11-plus and ended up at a secondary modern. This later became known as the

13-plus, and it meant that late developers, or children who, for some reason or other, had not done as well as they might in the 11-plus, could have another chance.

In fact, it was originally envisaged that some children who were given places at grammar schools would later be found to be unsuited to that style of academic education, just as there would be others who went on to secondary moderns who might be recognised by their teachers as grammar school material and consequently moved to the grammar school. This might have been the theory, but in practice it was a very rare event.

Me and a couple of friends passed the 11-plus and went to the local grammar. We felt out of place there and the masters weren't at all happy with our work. They used to say outright that we would probably do better at a secondary modern, and my parents were told so on open days. There didn't seem to be any method, though, that they could actually get rid of us, and we all three stayed there until we left at fifteen. I remember one or two boys coming to the grammar in the third year who had passed the 13-plus, but I never heard of it happening in the opposite direction; that is, grammar school boys moving to the secondary modern. (Glynn Mitchell)

Interestingly, although most people today have heard of the 11-plus, few seem to know about the 13-plus. There is a belief that once a child had failed the 11-plus, that was it. This was not the case at all.

Thank God for the 13-plus! I really messed up my 11-plus and thought that I was doomed to leave school at fifteen without any GCEs and work in a factory. However, the 13-plus came to my rescue and I was whisked out of the secondary modern and into the grammar. I have to say, without boasting, that I flourished there. I actually got more GCEs than almost anybody else in my class. If it hadn't been for the 13-plus though, I would have been stuck in a secondary modern without any chance at all of taking any sort of examination, apart perhaps from one in shorthand-typing. (Dorothy Dobson)

As a matter of fact, despite the best intentions of those who set up the system, no mechanism existed, apart from the 13-plus in some places, for putting right any mistake made in the allocation of secondary places following children taking the 11-plus. For most of them, there was one chance and that was it. Children who moved from one type of secondary school to another remained very much the exception, right the way through to the abolition of the selective system.

> Although my parents confidently expected me to pass the 11-plus, I didn't and wound up staying on the same site as my junior school, going to the secondary modern there. There was always a second chance for getting to the grammar school though, via the 'transfer' exam at thirteen. The head of my school was dead set against this, as he felt that this was an implied slur to his own school; that anybody would want to move to the grammar. He made a statement at assembly shortly before entries had to be made for the exam. He told us all that none of us were likely to pass the transfer, that we would, in any case, be happier here than at a grammar school and that the grammar school was no better than his secondary modern anyway. My parents were furious about this. I took the 13-plus anyway and passed, but it was no thanks to the head. (John B. Fleming)

> I took the 13-plus and not only passed it and went to the grammar, but did very well once I was there. I got good O level results and then stayed on for the sixth. I got a place at Warwick, the first person in my family to get to university. If it hadn't been for that second chance and the 13-plus, I would not have gone to university. (Dorothy Dobson)

Brian Simon observed that pupils who transferred from secondary moderns to Salford Grammar School at the age of thirteen often did better than those who had passed the 11-plus in the first place. He began to suspect that there might be many children languishing in secondary moderns who were perfectly capable of benefiting from the sort of education offered by grammar schools. Until the 1960s, pupils in secondary moderns were almost all barred from gaining any sort of qualification at all. Some secondary moderns experimented with arranging for their older pupils to sit GCEs and the results were very revealing. Those taking GCEs at secondary moderns seemed to do almost as well as those at grammar schools.

   In 1953, Brian Simon published a study of the 11-plus called 'Intelligence Testing and the Comprehensive School'. In this detailed critique of the methods then being used, Simon provided clear evidence that the main function of the 11-plus was, as many had suspected, not to single out those with superior intelligence, but to sort out the articulate middle-class children and provide them with grammar school places.

> I don't remember it being talked about, but I think everybody knew that there was a pretty straightforward connection between what your father did for a living and your chances of getting through the 11-plus. I noticed it in the first year at grammar school, which would have been in 1949; nearly all the boys were well spoken and their fathers had professional jobs or, at the very least, owned shops. There weren't any sons of labourers or road sweepers. As I moved up through the school, we did talk about it and I think we realised that there was something more to the business than us being clever. (Glynn Mitchell)

Even today, half a century or so after it was generally abandoned, there are still many people who view the days of widespread selective education in this country as a golden age.

Starting School

In Britain, during the years following the Second World War, there was a shake-up of secondary education, but for the younger children things did not really change. Starting school was still a major milestone.

Most small children in the late 1940s lived in traditional families, staying at home all day with their mothers while their fathers went out to work. The law required then, as it still does, that full-time education should begin in the term following a child's fifth birthday. In those days, this was when education truly did begin, often with little or no prior warning or preparation.

I had spent every single day with my mother until I was five. She took me shopping with her, we listened to 'Listen with Mother' with Daphne Oxenford on the wireless every afternoon at a quarter to two. 'This is the BBC Home Service for mothers and children at home.' Then the dingy-dong music, followed by Daphne Oxenford's beautiful voice saying, 'Are you sitting comfortably? Then I'll begin.' This delightful idyll came to an abrupt end on the Monday following my fifth birthday. I had been taken to the school to meet the headmistress and there had been some discussion about my attending, but, children being children, it didn't seem real to me until it actually happened. After that initial interview with the head, my mother did not set foot inside the infants' school again to my knowledge. There was a lych-gate shelter in the playground and my mother took me there on that awful morning and simply delivered me to a complete stranger. I felt utterly bereft and horribly betrayed! How could she just abandon me in that way? No more 'Listen with Mother' and trips to the shops; just being stuck all day with people I didn't even know. It was, I think, the biggest shock of my life. (Peter A. Barker)

I had spent odd days being looked after by friends of my mother from time to time and I didn't really understand the permanent nature of the arrangements being made for school. I tolerated the first day and then came home expecting my usual life in my mother's company to resume. I was terribly shocked when she told me that this excursion had not been a one-off, but was to become a regular feature of my life. I burst into tears and was absolutely inconsolable. (Lillian O. Drake)

I don't remember it myself, but my parents always told the story of what I supposedly said after my mother had collected me from school and taken me home after my first day there. Apparently, she sat me down and gave me some juice and biscuits, before asking me what I had thought of the experience. According to her, I said very judicially, 'Well I quite liked it, but I don't think I want to go again.' I don't remember actually saying this, but I do know that I didn't like going to the infants' school and would far rather have stayed at home with my mother. (Ronald G. Feeney)

Despite the often abruptness in which a child would begin their education, most children loved starting school.

I found life at home with my mother pretty dull. She was always busy and never seemed to have time to do anything with me. A lot of the time, I felt in the way. It wasn't really her fault; there was always so much to do. On Mondays, for instance, there was the washing. This was a full day's work for housewives then; the copper, scrubbing clothes on a washboard, rinsing them, putting them through the mangle – it must have been a nightmare trying to get all that done with two small children running round. I think that she was as pleased as we were when we started school. (Josephine A. Wilson)

I had never used paints before in my life. The paints were mixed with water in jam jars from big tins of powder. The colours were so vivid,

I can still remember the thrill of dipping the big, thick brush in the jar and making a vivid red slash across the paper. This was in the late 1940s and things were a bit bleak at that time. I even remember those days in shades of grey, like an old photograph. But the pictures that I painted in the infants, those are still bright, fresh and dazzling coloured. I had never done anything like that in my life before I started school. (Lillian O. Drake)

The post-war years were pretty grim in many ways. Homes didn't have as many luxuries as they do today, and it wasn't always easy to keep children entertained. Housework occupied mothers for a huge chunk of their time; with no labour-saving devices like washing machines and refrigerators for ordinary families, every day was an endless round of shopping, cleaning, washing and a hundred and one other tasks which ensured that the home was in good order.

There was very little to distract and entertain small children while all this was going on. Few televisions, no DVDs, computers; even record players were luxury items. What were pre-school children supposed to do while their mothers got on with the housework? For many mothers, the day that the youngest child started school might have been an occasion for tears, but in other cases it must have come as a blessed relief. Quite a few children too must have found it a novelty to be spending the day with adults who seemed to have all the time in the world to do things with them.

I thought starting school was the most exciting thing in the world. My brother and sister were at the juniors or 'big school' as we used to call it. Everything about school was new, strange and exciting. The things we did! Playing on the equipment in the hall, painting, having stories read to us; it was utterly magical. (Josephine A. Wilson)

By the time children start school today, they have already had so many different experiences that I don't think school can be anywhere near as exciting as it was when I started. All I really knew were the streets around our home. I had never seen a television, except in a shop window, never been to the pictures, and never been on holiday. All I knew was the little terrace house I grew up in. And, of course, a few other terraced houses. Never been to a funfair or held a paintbrush; the list of things I hadn't done would run to a dozen pages. For me, school was liberation from my day-to-day life, stuck indoors with my mother all day. (Lillian O. Drake)

In general, children start school today with a wide variety of experiences already under their belts. The majority are familiar with colour films and watch television regularly, and many have been to exciting places such as Legoland or Alton Towers.

Things were vastly different in 1945, and for some years after that. There might be a few toy soldiers, some plasticine, a few die-cast metal vehicles, but that would be about it. The only games in the house might be draughts, snakes and ladders; board games of that sort. Even if the mother had the time to spare, these games can be somewhat of an ordeal when played with the under-fives! Even if the family was well-off enough to have a television, there were no programmes on during the day. The first five years of a child's life could accordingly contain long stretches when there really was literally nothing to do. For children in homes of this sort, the great majority in fact, starting school was a pleasant surprise, with far more to interest and amuse them than they were likely to have at home.

I don't think that anybody today can possibly imagine how boring life was just after the war! Nobody seemed to have any money and there was nothing at all to do. Weekends were so deadly dull that after I started school, I used to long for Monday morning. When I grew up, my mother confided that she had felt exactly the same. (Josephine A. Wilson)

These were the days when parents were not even allowed to visit their children in hospital, because it was thought that they would upset the child and disrupt the smooth running of the ward. The thought of allowing parents into the infants' school to comfort and reassure their children when they were beginning full-time education simply would not have occurred to anybody. Nor would the mothers themselves have expected it.

I was literally plucked from my mother's arms for the first few days after I started school. She felt terrible, I'm sure, but no mother in those days would have thought of arguing with a teacher. If the teacher said that I was being silly and that the sooner my mother went home the better it would be for me, then that is what she had to do. I remember crying desolately for my mother after she had gone. The teacher wasn't cruel, just matter-of-fact and brisk. (Peter A. Barker)

These days, of course, children are eased gently into the whole routine of school, and parents are usually welcome to enter the premises. In the 1940s and '50s, the school and its grounds were very much the teachers' territory and they didn't want mothers cluttering up the place. This was a time when parents were learning that they had to trust the 'professionals' in many areas of their lives, not just education. For centuries, it had been the tradition that parents taught their children to read and write. This was now officially discouraged. New 'scientific' ways of teaching reading were becoming the vogue in classrooms, and foolish and misguided parents could irreparably damage their children's literacy by interfering in this process.

My mother and father had taught me to read as a matter of course. First they taught me the alphabet and then simple words. By the time I began at infants, I was able to read simple books. My first teacher was horrified and made a point of speaking to my mother about this. I got the impression that she saw parents teaching their own children as being little better than child abuse. My mother had to agree not to continue with her teaching, lest I was left with some unspecified lasting harm. She didn't stop of course and my father just laughed about it. It gives you some idea though of how people were feeling about teachers then. Teaching had always been a vocation, but now it had become a profession. Everything was to be done scientifically and parents should not have the temerity to think that they could be involved in the business. (Ronald G. Feeney)

I sometimes take my grandchildren to school and I can never get over the relaxed informality of the way parents and teachers talk to each other. It is nearly all Christian names these days and the mothers just wander into the playground, chatting with teachers and even wandering into the school itself when they come to collect their children. When I was at infants and junior school, my mother was not allowed to set foot past the school gate; as for speaking to the teacher, that was unheard of. You might get the chance once a term, although I don't even remember that when I was very little. Teachers were remote and important figures and parents took their word absolutely. (Dorothy Dobson)

For most children, starting school meant a step-change in the pace of their lives. Learning to read, for example:

I can still remember learning to read from *Janet and John* books. They began to be published a year or two before I started school and they were quite different from any of the books which had been used before for teaching five-year-olds to read. I know this because our infants had the old books alongside the new *Janet and John* ones. The older ones were dry and relied heavily upon rhymes and phonics. There were no pictures in them either. Just stuff like 'a pig in a wig did a jig'. *Janet and John* were something else. The first in the series was called *Here We Go* and had a yellow cover. They were paperbacks; not a common format in those days for school books. Instead of phonics, they relied upon the new method of 'Look and Say', where children learned whole words at once. Each simple sentence was accompanied by a bright, colour picture of the two children playing out of doors. 'Come here, John. Come here. See the little dog.' 'Look John, look.' (Josephine A. Wilson)

I could already read when I started school. When the teacher found out, she didn't look very pleased. With a large class all doing the same thing at the same time, it only needed one awkward customer like me to upset the entire system! Her solution was masterful; she decided to ignore my literacy entirely. I was made to learn the letter sounds just like my more ill-educated classmates and to work my way through the *Janet and John* books, starting with *Here We Go*. It was completely mad, because at home I was reading the newspaper in the evening! (Peter A. Barker)

Starting to read was one major milestone; the other was learning to write. This also began in the infants.

It will seem almost unbelievable, but when I began school in 1951 we were still using slates. Really, they were very practical for small children. We wrote on them with a pencil made of some sort of clay. The accepted way of cleaning the slate was to spit on it and then wipe it with your sleeve. (Lillian O. Drake)

Many schools, particularly those in rural districts, continued to use slates well into the 1950s. They were cheap and virtually indestructible under normal conditions. Certainly, they worked out a good deal cheaper than using paper. At the time there were no such things as felt-tip or roller-ball pens. In the schools which had abandoned the use of slates, the rule was that only pencils were to be used for the first few years of a child's school career. After this, they graduated to dip pens. Fountain pens were expensive; practically luxury items. A new fountain pen was the sort of thing which a child might receive as a birthday present.

The rule was that we could only use pencils and then when we went to 'big school' (the juniors) we would be allowed to use ink. There was some sense in this, because you would have to be pretty mad, even today, to let five- and six-year-olds anywhere near inkwells! (Mary Olive)

If we wanted to sharpen our pencils, then we had to go up to Miss Williams' desk. She had a rotary pencil sharpener clamped to the side of her desk; the sort where one had to turn a handle to sharpen the pencil. Breaking the point of one's pencil was regarded as carelessness, and you got told off if you had to sharpen your pencil more than once in a day. (Ronald G. Feeney)

A couple of weeks before the end of the term when I was due to leave infants, our teacher decided as a treat to let us try writing with real pens. The excitement! We had only used pencils and slates up to that point, and she thought that it would be a good idea if we got the feel of writing with a pen before we started juniors. She handed out dip pens with wooden handles; the sort of thing Bob Cratchit writes with in *A Christmas Carol*. Then she filled the white porcelain inkwells with something like a miniature watering can full of ink. Of course, it took a while to get the hang of it, but I was so proud to be able to go home that day and tell my mother that we had been doing 'real' writing! (Dorothy Dobson)

Dip pens were still in use in many primary schools until well into the 1960s. The position of ink monitor, the person responsible for ensuring that the inkwells in the desks were kept topped up, was the first post to which many children aspired. Only the steadiest and most reliable children would be chosen for this job, entailing as it did filling up tiny cans like those which we use today to water houseplants. It was no job for a careless or lively child, as spilling a can of ink would be a major disaster.

> I was ink monitor and it was my job to make sure that all the inkwells were kept topped up. I was a very neat and careful little girl, but even the most careful child can have a mishap. I was carrying the ink can one day, when I tripped up and the ink went everywhere. The teacher was very nice about it; she knew that it was pure accident, but you can have no idea just how much mess a quarter of a pint of ink can make. The floor of the classroom was wooden and the stains remained even after the mess had been mopped up by the caretaker. Every time I passed that spot, I felt guilty and ashamed. (Josephine A. Wilson)

> One of my ambitions at juniors was to be ink monitor. In retrospect, I can see that there was not the remotest chance of my ever having been appointed to this post. I was very well behaved, but abnormally clumsy. The idea of being entrusted with a little can of ink would have been a recipe for disaster. It required a steady hand and an ability to walk round the class slowly and carefully without being liable to drop things or fall over. (Gregory Parker)

The writing skills being taught to children in 1945 had remained unchanged for centuries. One had to dip the pen in the inkwell after every word or two, and if you were not careful you could end up making a frightful mess. The problem was that the ink took quite a while to dry, and unless you were incredibly careful you would end up with a lot of splodges and smears. Of course, it took quite some time to get the hang of writing with such a pen. Dip the nib in the inkwell, remove excess ink on the inside edge of the inkwell and then write a word or two. Use blotting paper when necessary; for instance if you wanted to turn the page to carry on writing. There is a knack to writing with a dip pen. Make your strokes in the wrong way and the nib will twist and spray minute droplets of ink on the page. This sort of thing does not go down well with the teacher; it makes your work look messy. Used properly and carefully, writing with a dip pen should be as neat as that done with a biro.

After I left juniors, I was allowed to keep some of my exercise books. The writing in them is really beautiful; nothing at all like the way I write these days! There was something about using a dip pen that made you take extra care. If you fought against the nib, tried to push it in the wrong direction, then it would judder and spray a mist of tiny ink droplets about. You learned very early on how to guide it round the curves of the letters. Also, because you could only write a word at a time before dipping your pen in the inkwell, you thought more about what you were doing. You couldn't scribble with a dip pen the way you can with a biro. Every movement has to be careful and controlled. (Dorothy Dobson)

Biros, for some strange reason, were absolutely prohibited at school. Of course, in the first few years after the end of the war they were horribly expensive. A ballpoint pen cost about £3 in 1947, equivalent to around £80 today. Even as late as 1970, in an age when ballpoint pens were mass produced cheaply and regarded as being disposable, many schools maintained a ban upon their use. This applied to both primary and secondary schools.

I remember doing a piece of homework in biro. My teacher returned it to me later in the day with two red lines through it. I had to do it again. I don't know to this day what the objection was to ballpoints, unless it was just because they were new and modern. (Ellen T. Cade)

We could only use real ink; either dip pens or fountain pens. There was a blanket ban on ballpoints for schoolwork. Part of it might have been that when we were learning to write, we were taught to make some strokes in our handwriting thick and some thin. It was a variation of the old copper plate. Now you can produce that sort of writing with a proper nib, it's a question of making a broad stroke or turning the nib sideways and using the edge. It does look beautiful when properly done and you definitely can't do it with a biro. Maybe that was the reason, to maintain that style of handwriting. (Glynn Mitchell)

Biros were banned. I don't know if it was just that they were something new or that the writing you produced with them looked a bit spidery and thin compared with what you could do with a proper pen, but they were not allowed at all. I got the feeling that the teachers were a bit snobbish about them; respectable people wrote with proper pens, not some strange new contraption invented by a foreigner. (James R. Harker)

At a time when the majority of homes lacked an inside lavatory, it was no surprise that they were also outside at schools. Incredibly, many of them had no roofs, and so paper was not left in them; it had to be carried out across the playground for every excursion. Asking to be excused and knowing that others were watching how many sheets of paper one took could be a torment for some children.

On my first day of school, I suffered the catastrophe of wetting my knickers. I was always very embarrassed about anything to do with going to the toilet. Even at home, I hated any mention of it. When I started school, I could not bring myself to ask where the lavatory was. I looked around surreptitiously, but could see no door anywhere which might be the place. The only door which might have been the right one was the staff room. I only worked this out because I saw grown-ups coming and going through it. It simply did not occur to me that the low, brick building on the far side of the playground could have anything to do with it. It looked far too big. And so, in the end, when I couldn't hold it any more, the inevitable happened. I think that this was the worst thing which ever happened to me in childhood. (Dorothy Dobson)

The toilet paper used at that time was like nothing anybody sees today. It was hard, translucent and scratchy; very similar to tracing paper. Indeed, it was sometimes used for this purpose. Of course, it was completely un-absorbent and very uncomfortable to use. (Ellen T. Cade)

After asking to be excused we had to go to the teacher's table for the paper. You could tell by the number of sheets taken whether somebody was going to do number ones or number twos, as we put it then. It was a degrading ritual, having to ask first for permission to visit the toilet and then to have people watching how many sheets of paper you needed. (John B. Fleming)

For some, even commonplace events proved a novelty.

Of course, we didn't have a television at home, but we didn't have a radio either. Nor did we have any books at home. When I started school, I had never heard of such a thing as a fairy story. My whole life up to the age of five had been practical and full only of real and solid things. My parents were not imaginative and I don't think it ever occurred to them to tell me stories. When I started school, everything was wonderful and new. I particularly loved story time. This was at the end of the afternoon, when all the hustle and bustle was over and we were all feeling tired. For half an hour, we would all sit on the mat and listen to Miss Bates, the teacher, reading us a story. I started school in the autumn and there was no central heating in the school, which was a draughty old Victorian one. Instead, each classroom had an open fire and the caretaker used to come round with a scuttle and put coal on when it was needed. We sat on a mat by the fire while Miss Bates read us fairy stories and, believe it or not, on one occasion *Little Black Sambo*! For a child who had never heard anything fantastic and who didn't even know what magic was supposed to be, those story sessions were a revelation. Of all my experiences at school, they have remained the most vivid and exciting. (John B. Fleming)

Since most infant and junior schools were on the same site, it was inevitable that the reputations of the children moving up into the juniors would precede them; which were the 'nice' children, who was rowdy and rough, which ones were likely to benefit from a more intensive education. The teachers, often from more educated backgrounds than the families of the children who they taught, might well have been expected to favour children who were well behaved, polite and spoke grammatically correct English.

I don't know to this day what the criteria were for ending up in the A stream at juniors. I know that I went straight into it and I am also aware that others who had been at infants in the same year as me went directly into the B and C classes, which virtually guaranteed them a place at the secondary modern. There were no proper tests in the infants and the whole education was fairly informal, so I can only guess how they decided which children were worth teaching intensively in the A stream. Most of those in the A stream were like me and came from a slightly better sort of home. Our parents didn't work in factories or building sites. I can't think that that was all there was to it, but I really don't know how it worked. (Peter A. Barker)

The A streams of both primary and secondary schools provided completely different educations, geared to very different ends. In primary school, the stream that a child was in was a pretty accurate prediction of whether or not he was likely to pass the 11-plus, while in a grammar school, the children who were in the A stream were being groomed for university, while those in the B and C streams were expected to leave at fifteen or sixteen. Therefore, being in one stream or the other had profound effects upon a child's future; it could, in effect, decide the whole future course of his or her life.

> I remember when we moved from infants, there was some sort of test. It wasn't made very much of and none of us realised the importance of it, but a week or two later we were allocated our classes. I was in 1C. As I moved up through the juniors, I kind of absorbed an almost fatalistic attitude towards the 11-plus. Those of us in 4C were simply not expected to pass it, and I didn't. (Ronald G. Feeney)

There was no streaming in the infants' schools, although some quarters believed that there should be. Sometimes, within a couple of months of starting school at around the age of five, already the idea of who was likely to do well and who was probably going to be a slow learner was becoming fixed in the heads of the teachers. None of these decisions were communicated to either parents or children, so no appeal was possible, but children were being sorted and categorised from the moment they first set foot in school.

> My mother was an awful snob, but in a funny kind of way it paid off. She felt that she was better than the other mothers in our street and didn't mind showing it. She spoke better than most of them. When I started school, she didn't chat to the other mums waiting outside, but when she bumped into my teacher in the shops, she made a point of talking to her in a friendly way. I don't know if that made any difference, but I was something of a pet of the teacher, Miss Sharp. Somehow, this business of being teacher's pet continued into the next class and at primary school. I can't help thinking that it had

something to do with the fact that the teachers thought of me as being a slightly higher social class than the other girls in the class. Anyway, I was in the A stream all the way through school and passed the 11-plus without too much difficulty. (Peter A. Barker)

This sort of informal process, whereby some children became favourites of the teacher because their parents seemed to be the 'right' sort of people, could have a tremendous impact upon the path of the child's education.

When children turned seven they would be transferred to junior school, often known as the 'big school'. It was in those years – age seven up to age eleven – that the futures of many children became decided by the stream into which they were placed. In the next chapter, we shall look in detail at the way in which this operated, and why some children were more or less assured at this stage in their education of a place in a grammar school, while others were consigned to secondary moderns.

Primary School

Upon starting juniors at primary school, children found themselves assigned to different streams and it was this assignment which would be greatly influential on whether or not they would pass the all-important 11-plus. Those in the A streams received harder work and specialised coaching in the skills which they would need in order to do well on 'scholarship day', as the day when the 11-plus was taken was more commonly known. Once in the A stream, children received more attention from the teachers and as a result performed better academically. Conversely, those in the B and C streams received less tuition and so inevitably failed to make strong progress. By the time that these children had reached the fourth year of juniors, what we now call Year 6, the chances of anybody not in the A stream passing the 11-plus were slim.

I found myself in 2B at primary school. In theory, children could move up into the A class if they were in a B. So too could those in an A slip down and be demoted to a B or C. In practice, this never happened. At least, I never saw it happen. Once they had decided that you were clever, a bit slow but tried hard or completely thick, that was it. You were labelled for good! You went into an A, B or C class and everybody knew what to expect of you. Although I was in 4B when I took the 11-pus, I somehow passed. I didn't get the impression that my teacher was particularly pleased about it. I think she felt that somehow this undermined her professional judgement. Children in 4B and 4C weren't supposed to do that. (Keith J. Ballard)

But how was it decided who was clever enough to be in the A stream? Of course, things were a lot more competitive then and children were constantly tested on their academic ability, with their cumulative scores being marked on a report at the end of each term. Presumably, this would enable an accurate estimate of a child's intellect. However, there were two concerning factors surrounding this. Firstly, classes at the time were so large that it was almost impossible for a teacher to have a detailed knowledge of the strengths and weaknesses of every one of the pupils in their charge.

Believe it or not, there were just over fifty children in the class I was in at junior school. This was in 1948 or 1949. Just one teacher as well, no helpers or classroom assistants in those days. Somehow, she had to keep order and supervise our education. Inevitably, some of the quieter children ended up being ignored. I'm sure that there were some very bright kids in the class, but there were just so many of us that it was easy for some of them to be over looked. This was especially so if they were the sort who came across as being a little slow. The teacher only had a certain amount of time and preferred to spend it on those she was reasonably sure would get through the 11-plus. I don't blame her, but it was a bit hard on those who didn't seem worth her attention. (Gregory Parker)

There were never fewer than forty children in any class I was in at primary school. More often it was forty-five or fifty. The only way that one woman – teachers were nearly always women – could keep control was by being very strict and not allowing any cheek or naughtiness. Teachers certainly had their favourites, children that they were more concerned with than others. These were the ones that were given special help. I suppose it was inevitable really, teachers were only human. The ones our teacher seemed to really take to were the polite, well-spoken ones. I don't know if they were really brighter than the rest of us, but I'm sure they were more of a pleasure to work with! I'm afraid I wasn't one of her favourites and she seemed content to leave me to my own devices for a lot of the time. (Dorothy Dobson)

Some pupils were, in a sense, marked out for success and expected by both the school and their parents to pass the 11-plus. A natural corollary of course is that if some were picked for success, then others were in the same way marked for failure. In the meantime, it must be said that life at primary school at that time could be a lot of fun.

I grew up in the East End of London. It was a rough area and when I was in the juniors, the teachers all lived nearby the school. Hardly anybody had cars in those days, which was about 1950, I suppose. One young woman, very well educated, she had come to work in that part of London because she believed that that was where she could do most good in the world. I didn't know that at the time of course, it is what I heard later after I had left school. Anyway, she cadged tickets from concert halls and even the Colosseum in the West End. In her own time at weekends and in the evenings she took groups of us to classical music concerts and even the opera. It opened up a whole new world to kids who would otherwise never have gone to such places. I suppose these days you would need to do all manner of risk assessments and have a CRB check to arrange trips like that. (Lillian O. Drake)

Of course there was no National Curriculum in those days and the teachers often taught what they pleased. Obviously we had to learn arithmetic and English, but apart from that, the various form teachers we had at junior school all had completely different ideas about what was important for us to learn. One was mad keen on what we called 'nature study'. There was a nature table with a bird's nest, sheep's skull, old wasps' nest, fossils, shells and all sorts of other things on it. This teacher, Miss Williams, used to take us out to the park collecting specimens and looking at flowers and trees. Another teacher we had was hot on art and we did a lot of sculpting in clay and papier-mâché. Also trips to art galleries and painting outdoors. I loved the juniors and for the first few years of secondary school felt almost bereaved at the loss of that style of learning. (Ronald G. Feeney)

During the 1940s and '50s, teachers had a huge amount of leeway in what they taught the children in their care. However, grammar schools took a slightly different approach to teaching. Their aim was to put as many children as possible through as many exams as could be managed. Grammar schools were judged by how many of their pupils passed the School Certificate or Higher School Certificate. In secondary moderns things were more laid-back, since there was no question of the pupils taking any examinations. Often, the transition from primary to secondary modern did not result in a noticeably different style of teaching; the secondary moderns closely resembled the old all-age elementary schools, which were supposed to have been abolished.

> In retrospect, the years I spent at primary school really were the happiest of my life. We had got over the trauma of being taken from our mothers to spend the day with a random collection of strangers, and by the time we entered the juniors at seven, those people had become friends and acquaintances. We were all called by our Christian names and the atmosphere was very cosy. (Dorothy Dobson)

> The transition from primary to secondary school went almost unnoticed by many of us. The secondary school was on the same site, in fact in the same building. I didn't see much difference in what we were being taught either, to be honest. It was a pretty smooth process, we moved from infants to juniors and then on to the secondary modern, and in each case it only meant moving a few yards either sideways or upwards. I know that when my own kids went to school, there was a big disruption when they started secondary school; a step change, you might call it. There was none of this feeling when I was at school. It was just one continuous process, with not much difference at any stage. (Gregory Parker)

There were no educational league tables at the time, and yet some primary schools were certainly regarded as being better than others. They were the ones which managed to get a lot of children into grammar schools. The teachers in such schools took pride in their success rate and tended to focus on those children who seemed most likely to be able to pass the 11-plus.

> I was in the A stream all the way through juniors, and most of the kids who were in the same class with me passed the 11-plus. Even at the time I thought there was something a bit fishy about the streaming. For one thing, the children in my class, the A class,

seemed to have parents who were professionals or at the very least white-collar clerical workers. The fathers of my friends at primary school included the local doctor, a solicitor and an accountant. I don't remember any of the fathers being Dockers or factory workers. Years later, I read Aldous Huxley's *Brave New World* and it put me very strongly in mind of this. We were the 'Alphas' and those in the C classes were the 'Epsilon minuses'! Another odd thing was that my friends and I seemed to be taller and better built than those in the B and C classes. It wasn't only academically that we did well; we dominated Sport's Day as well. (Peter A. Barker)

Those in the A class at juniors almost seemed like a different species to us! They were certainly bigger and often spoke 'posh'. The teachers had more time for them and they were less likely to get into trouble than us in B. Mind you, we were a cut above the C class, where the kids came from really rough families and some of them could barely read. When you're a kid you take all this for granted, but I'm quite sure now that by the third or fourth year at juniors we had all been put into neat categories for our future lives. The A pupils would be going to the grammar school and getting good jobs; us in B would perhaps be in shops or offices, and the Cs would be digging the roads! Like I say, I didn't think this at the time; it's just noticing how things turned out later. (Ronald G. Feeney)

The fact is that well-behaved children received, on a whole, more attention and tutoring than those children who were rougher, cheekier and more mischievous. This inevitably had a knock-on effect educationally.

I was in 2B at juniors and then, because I was doing so well, I was moved up into 3A. I noticed the difference at once. In 2B the teacher had given us a lot of craft activities and not pushed us very hard at sums. In 3A we were expected to work hard, and my new teacher, Miss Bradley, was constantly reminding us that we would be sitting the 11-plus the next year. A lot of the work focused on the skills that we would need for the 11-plus; composition writing, long division, things like that. Everything changed once I was in the A class. In 2B we might have been set a composition called, say, 'A day at the Seaside'. In 3A it was more things like 'What I would do if I was Prime Minister'.

We were made to think in the A class, rather than just being allowed to coast along. (Keith J. Ballard)

Those of us in the A classes were definitely treated as something of an elite. Our teachers would encourage this feeling by telling us about how different we were from the other streams. I remember once our class teacher doing some multiplication sums with us. She pointed out that this was really just a quicker way of adding up. Then she said, 'Of course that's what they do in 3B, they add everything up rather than multiply.' The impression one got was that she was very pleased to be working with bright sparks like us, rather than being stuck with those dunderheads in 3B. It made us feel good that she would confide in us like this, and I for one redoubled my efforts at maths so as to justify her good opinion of us. It wasn't a very professional way to carry on, but it made us eager to please her by getting the sums right. (Peter A. Barker)

At the time, researchers interested in how the 11-plus system worked highlighted the discrepancies in the selection process for the streams. Hilde Himmelweit, for example, stated:

In the teacher's view, the middle-class boy, taken all round, proves a more satisfying and rewarding pupil. He appears to be better mannered, more industrious, more mature and even more popular than his working-class co-pupil.

D.F. Swift, a well-known sociologist and Professor of Educational Studies at the Open University from 1970 to 1986, had this to say:

The basic facts of social class performance in school are so well known as hardly to need repeating. As all teachers know, the children who do the best work are easiest to control and stimulate, make the best prefects, stay at school longest, finish school with the best qualifications and references, and get into the best jobs, tend to come from the middle class.

In other words, when children entered the juniors, some teachers there already had a good idea in their own minds which of them would be likely to pass the 11-plus and go on to grammar school. It was these children who were already marked out for success in the eyes of the staff at the primary school.

> I suppose that I was something of a teacher's pet when I was in the juniors. Something I noticed was that our teacher in the first and second years was a lot nicer to me and half a dozen others than she was to the rest of the form. We got made monitors, were asked to help out at things and generally got the feeling that she liked us. All of us who she treated like that passed our 11-plus and went on to grammar school. It was only in later years that it struck me that we were all nicely spoken and polite children from 'good' homes. I can't help thinking that this is why she seemed to take a particular interest in us. (Peter A. Barker)

Still, it might be argued, did this make any real difference? Surely the marks awarded in tests would have been evaluated without reference to matters of background and class? How could the attitude of the teachers have been responsible for getting all those middle-class children into the A streams at primary school? All the available evidence indicates that this prejudice on the part of teachers is quite sufficient by itself to explain why working-class children were funnelled into the B and C streams. Let us remind ourselves what was said by the former pupil above who was in an A class: 'It made us feel good that she would confide in us like this, and I for one redoubled my efforts at maths so as to justify her good opinion of us.'

What is known by psychologists as 'positive reinforcement' can have a very powerful effect on learning. In general, children will strive far harder to secure praise than they will to avoid censure. This in itself is probably sufficient to explain why the well mannered and polite children, upon whom such attentions were focused, tended to succeed academically. Experiments carried out in the 1960s provided evidence that this factor alone might be able to explain a lot about what was happening in British schools during this time.

In 1964, a researcher called Robert Rosenthal from Harvard University conducted a fascinating experiment in the American equivalent of a primary school. He selected various children, completely at random, and then told their teachers that this group had been scientifically identified as being 'late bloomers' – children who would, in the next few months, have tremendous spurts of academic achievement. Not surprisingly, the attitude of the teachers to these children changed and they became more positive about them. What was astonishing was that when tested a year later, the IQs of these children had actually soared, increasing far more than the other children in the year.

So what was happening? How could informing the teachers that the children were of above average intelligence result in an objectively measured increase in intellectual ability? The more positive reinforcement they received, the more they learned.

> I desperately wanted to be praised by Mrs Jenkins, our teacher. Like others in the class, I worked very hard to please her and elicit her congratulations, rather than because I was interested in sums or compositions. I wanted to be told what a clever girl I was. (Sheila Fawcett)

> By the third year at juniors, when I was ten, I had become a terrible creep. I would do anything to please teachers and they all thought I was such a lovely child. Part of this was making sure that all my work was done neatly and as best I could. This stood me in good stead during the 11-plus, of course. I think that our teachers encouraged this sort of sucking up and that they knew that if the children were trying hard to please them then they would work all the harder. (Peter A. Barker)

Those teachers who had classes formed from children streamed into A were more likely to have their charges go on to grammar school, which was a very satisfactory outcome of their job. On the other hand, for those who were in charge of classes from the B or C streams there was far less job satisfaction, as their pupils were unlikely to pass their 11-plus. Therefore, they had little incentive to coax, praise and encourage the pupils. Their professional status was seen to be lower than that of the teachers of the A classes and they were more often than not stuck with children who they believed would never be likely to amount to much in the world. It was not uncommon for children who ended up at grammar school to go back and visit their primary school teacher and thank them; it was, however, unusual for those who went to secondary moderns to do so.

> I never thought that our teachers at primary school cared much about how we got on. I'm not saying they were cruel or neglectful,

nothing like that. It was more that they didn't stretch us with the work and didn't seem to be pleased when we made a special effort. I was in the C class all through juniors and I know that some of the children practically worshiped their teachers. Thinking back, this was mainly those in the A classes. They formed a strong attachment to their teachers. One reason that didn't happen with us was that we had a lot of temporary people in, students and so on. It wasn't uncommon for us to have three teachers in one year and so we didn't really get a chance to bond with them. I can't help wondering if being given 3C wasn't like a penal posting, something which had to be endured rather than enjoyed. (Harry R. Smith)

Sixty years ago, typical classrooms in primary schools were very different to what we are used to today. For one thing, this was years before the idea of child-centred education and open-plan classrooms came to be generally accepted. School desks were arranged in orderly rows, all facing the front of the class, where the teacher would sit on a raised stage. Behind the teacher was the blackboard. Most lessons consisted of the children working quietly at their desks without talking to each other.

I remember getting the ruler for talking in class. I had only asked how to spell a word, but it was enough to count as disruptive behaviour. I had to go to the front of the class and hold out my hand so that I could be struck twice on the palm with a long wooden ruler. It stung rather than hurt, but it discouraged us from talking and made sure that we got on with our work. (Ronald G. Feeney)

I don't think that modern classroom methods would have worked in the old junior schools. Imagine having fifty children aged eight or nine milling about a room with just one adult to maintain order and teach them. It simply wouldn't work. Keeping us all sitting at our desks and not allowing much talking was the only way that any work would get done. (Dorothy Dobson)

The old-style desks, with their sloping lid and inkwell, were to be found in every school in the land, and were modelled on the sort of thing one might find in the scriptorium of a monastery; the place where illuminated manuscripts were copied. These desks had a number of advantages when used for large groups of restless and fidgety children. Many of the modern-day distractions within a classroom were obviated by the old desks. There were no chairs to scrape and lean back on; just an integral seat attached to the desk itself. These seats too were based on an ecclesiastical design; they were copies of the hinged seats found in old choir stalls.

> We didn't really have any choice but to sit still without fidgeting. The fold-up seat meant that there was no chair to shift about and no arguments about who we sat next to. The desks only had room for two, so there was never any question of groups of children gathering together to create mischief. I helped out in a school with my grand-children a few years ago and I can hardly tell you how much things had changed; groups of children talking about what they'd seen on television last night, three or four adults trying to move from place to place and get the children to get on with their work. And the noise! A constant bedlam of talking, shouting, chairs scraping, things being dropped. A wonder they manage to get anything at all done. (Dorothy Dobson)

> There's no doubt at all in my mind that the old-fashioned desks made it easier for the children to get on with their work. There simply wasn't any scope for mucking about, even in a minor way. The most you could get up to was talking to your neighbour and that was quickly dealt with by the teacher. Working under those conditions might not be a lot of fun, but you would get things done. You would have a class of nine-year-olds all sitting quietly, getting on with their writing. If you wanted to attract the teacher's attention, you had to hold your hand up in silence until she noticed you. (Sheila Fawcett)

In fact, the atmosphere in some of these classrooms would have been exactly like that of a scriptorium in a monastery, with the only sound being the scratching of the dip pens as children copied work from the blackboard. It is hard today to imagine a room with over fifty young children, all of whom had access to an inkwell, none of whom purposly spilled ink, splashed each other or generally played the fool. It would have been a foolhardy child indeed who dared to mess around in that way.

You read in books about ink pellets and so on, but I never saw anybody muck about with ink. The retribution would have been swift and severe. In all my time at primary school, I never saw anybody misuse the ink. The whole aim in those days was to get on with your work carefully and quietly without distracting others or making the teacher cross. We used to make up for it at playtime with a lot of charging around and shouting, but having got that out of our system for twenty minutes or so, we returned to the classroom and then worked in silence for perhaps an hour. (Keith J. Ballard)

It's hard to imagine now, with the way that children behave, but in the years after the war, classrooms in primary schools would be absolutely silent when the children were working. Not just for the odd minute, but for half an hour or more. The kids would all be sitting quietly, writing in their books, and you could hear nothing but the ticking of the clock on the wall at the back. I can tell you how quiet the children were because even when we were allowed to talk, one teacher said that she still wanted to be able to hear a pin drop. She meant this quite literally and she actually had a pin that she dropped from shoulder height to the floor. If she couldn't hear it hit the ground, then she said that the noise was getting too much. If we didn't quieten down, then she dropped the pin again. If she didn't hear it this time, then we had to stop talking altogether for half an hour and work in complete silence. (James H. Schneider)

By the fourth year in juniors, most children had a pretty good idea of where they stood in the scheme of things. If you were in a B or C class, then your fate was almost certainly to go to a secondary modern. This could also happen of course with those in the A class, but it was less likely. To be in the A class meant that you were likely grammar school material, and after four years of streaming, you knew it.

In our class, which was 4A, there were a bunch of us who all expected to go to the grammar. Some of us had brothers and sisters there, all of us were well spoken and lived in semi-detached houses. I only really used to associate with this group. From time to time, I visited the home of somebody not in this circle and I was often shocked at what I found. Some lived in tenement blocks or shared houses with other families. There seemed to me to be something very strange about a family who didn't have an entire house to themselves. All but one of my circle of friends passed the 11-plus. I don't believe I ever again had any dealings with any child whose parents didn't have a whole house to themselves. It's funny when you think about it, but the connection between living in semi-detached houses and passing the 11-plus didn't strike me at the time. I'm pretty sure now though that it was nearly always the ones from nice homes, at least in our school, that got through the 11-plus and went to grammar schools. (Peter A. Barker)

I was in A classes all the way through primary school. After 2A it was clear that the As were my natural home. Our teachers would talk about the two local grammar schools as though it was pretty certain that most of us would be going to one or the other. A lot of us had older brothers or sisters at them and so it all seemed to be pretty well fixed up. I don't recall ever questioning the fact that I would be going to the county high, it was just one of those things that one took for granted. (Conrad Summerfield)

Of course, the four years that children spent at the juniors was not wholly taken up with preparations for the 11-plus. For many, the years that they spent at primary school were the most enjoyable days of their school lives. But over it all loomed the shadow of that all-important examination. There were no educational league tables in the 1940s and '50s, but it was widely known that some primary schools were better than others; some schools had a reputation for getting children through the 11-plus and into grammar schools.

I remember that there were three primary schools more or less equidistant from my home. One was Catholic and so that was out. One of the others was on the edge of a rough district and right next door to the secondary modern. They had a very close relationship with the secondary modern and I have an idea that it was thought most of them would go there as a matter of course. The other school was by itself and this was where those whose parents wanted them to get on were sent. Most of the children who went to grammar school attended either this one or the Catholic school. (Josephine A. Wilson)

Children at primary schools were invariably called by their Christian names, and although they were expected to do as they were told promptly, the atmosphere was a lot more relaxed and easygoing than it was in secondary schools. The contrast when children left primary school could be sharp and many children looked back nostalgically for the days when they were in the juniors.

> In the juniors, we were always called John or Peter. As soon as I started at the grammar, that all changed. There it was Carter or Williams. I don't think that I was ever addressed by any teacher other than by my surname for all the five years that I was at secondary school. I believe that this changed once one was in the sixth form, but for the rest of the school it was surnames only. This felt cold and harsh compared with the way that our teachers spoke to us in the juniors. I know it will sound feeble, but for the first year or two in the grammar, I used to long to be back in the juniors. It was like a lost golden age! (Peter A. Barker)

> Although of course we did harder work in the juniors than we did in infants, there were still times when we relaxed and just enjoyed ourselves. Games like rounders were not really competitive in the juniors; we just played for fun. Once you hit secondary school though, it was all teams and houses and every game was an ordeal. You didn't run round the field for the exercise; you played to win. In the juniors, right up to the fourth year, our teachers would sometimes let us all cluster round them while they read us a story. Nothing like that happened once you were in secondary school. I really missed the juniors. (Keith J. Ballard)

There is no doubt that the transition from primary to secondary could be something of a culture shock for children in those days. Suddenly being addressed by one's surname must have come as a surprise for some boy who had always been called Timmy or John up to that point. The use of first names for children at school today is almost universal in both primary and secondary.

The transition from primary or junior school to secondary was likely to prove more of a trial for those passing the 11-plus than for those who went to secondary moderns, particularly in the years immediately following the end of the Second World War. This was because grammar schools existed, as they always had done, in separate physical locations from primary schools. For historic reasons at which we have already looked, this was not the case with many secondary modern schools; which were often on the same site as the primary school.

> I did not find leaving primary school and moving to the secondary a wrench or even a change. After all, Jubilee Street infants, juniors and secondary modern were all in the same building, so I already knew the teachers and many of the pupils at the secondary school by sight long before I left the juniors. Primary school was not really distinct from secondary, just on another floor in the same building. (Lorna Gavin)

For others, the change at the end of primary school was dramatic – one might almost be tempted to say traumatic.

> For the first year after leaving primary school, I used to go back every few weeks to visit the place. The grammar school was so harsh and business-like compared with those days in the juniors, that I felt quite bereft. I was not the only one either. Apart from anything else, the juniors I went to was mixed and that was pleasant. The teachers were nearly all women at that time in primary schools, whereas in the grammar they were all men. The contrast between primary and secondary could hardly have been greater. (Paul M. Richardson)

Introducing the 11-plus

Despite its general abolition almost half a century ago, the 11-plus examination still casts an exceedingly long shadow. There are many, including former Deputy Prime Minister John Prescott and pop singer Cliff Richard, who still feel the sting of what they saw as failure to pass this most controversial of examinations. Even today, there is still furious debate regarding the supposed virtues and alleged shortcomings of the selective education scheme which operated in this country for twenty years or so following the end of the Second World War.

Of course, strictly speaking there should have been no question of anybody 'failing' the 11-plus. Its stated aim was merely to distinguish those children likely to benefit from a more academic education and ensure that they received it. From the beginning, the claim was that there would be 'parity of esteem' between grammar schools and the new secondary moderns.

I can still remember to this day, sixty-five years later, the sick dread with which I approached school on the morning of 'scholarship day'. That was what it was usually called in the early years; scholarship day. I don't remember hearing the expression 11-plus until some years later. My parents had left me in no doubt at all that this was the single most important day in my life and that how I performed that day would affect my entire future. That's a hell of a burden to put on a ten-year-old. They had been drilling me for months beforehand in writing compositions, practising sums and answering questions about things that they got me to read. The consequence was that all that I encountered was already familiar to me. When I got home, I was cross-examined about how it had gone and what sort of questions there had been. Oddly enough, I wasn't really that worried after taking the thing; I was pretty sure that I had passed. I was right, and there was great rejoicing in the house when the letter came. (Peter A. Barker)

Theoretically, the 11-plus was supposed to be an objective test, which would show the level of a child's intelligence. The claim was made that it was impossible to coach for this sort of test and that its results had nothing to do with previous education. Both the recollections of those who took and administered the 11-plus, together with later academic research, suggests otherwise.

I was in the C class at primary school. We were given work that was much easier than those in the A class. They were given a lot of extra practice as scholarship day approached. We had the feeling that it was more or less taken for granted that none of us in 4C had much chance. They were right. Nobody in my class passed. When I grew up, I heard the expression 'a self-fulfilling prophecy'. This struck me as the perfect description of what was going on. (Roanld G. Feeney)

I remember clearly sitting the 11-plus, despite the fact that it was over sixty years ago. The main thing I remember was the sense of unfairness. Everybody said that it was just an intelligence test and that it didn't matter which school you went to; if you were bright enough you would get through it okay. As soon as I looked at the papers, I knew, young as I was, that this wasn't true. I simply hadn't been taught some of the things that they were asking questions about. I remember vividly a question about prime factors. Now I knew what a prime number was and we had even done some work in class about something called the 'Sieve of Eratosthenes', which was designed to sort out prime numbers. But what on earth was a prime factor? I had no idea at all. A lot of the arithmetic questions were like that, stuff that we simply hadn't covered at school. I think that I knew then that the whole thing was a bit of a cheat and that however clever I was, I wasn't going to be able to pass this because the teachers hadn't taught us the right things. (Harry R. Smith)

The following are examples of questions taken from the 11-plus examination:

    i.   Simplify 7,236 X 5,287
    ii.   An aeroplane flies from Glasgow to London in 1 hour 51 minutes at 220 miles per hours. Find the distance in miles
    iii.   Write down the prime factors of 210

It is immediately apparent that questions like this have little to do with intelligence and everything to do with previous education. In other words, those who were in the top class of a good primary school would be far more likely to be able to answer them than anybody else. Those who had not received an efficient education or extra help from their parents would be absolutely stumped.

> The first sum was to multiply two long numbers by each other. We hadn't even been taught long multiplication in our class. The teacher had encouraged us to add up numbers rather than multiplying them. If we wanted to find the cost of seven items at £4 7s 6d each, we would just add them all together to find the amount. In the A class they were taught to put the amount at the top of a sum and then multiply by seven. A lot of the sums in the 11-plus were like that. We simply hadn't been shown how to do them at school. No wonder all the kids in my class failed! (John B. Fleming)

The examination itself was pretty tough and, contrary to all the assertions being made at the time, it was quite possible to coach children to get through it. Whatever it was that was being measured, it was certainly not natural intelligence! (The answers to the above questions are as follows: i. 38,256,732 ii. 407 miles iii. 2, 3, 5 and 7.)

Looking back with the perspective of sixty or seventy years, it seems more than a little bizarre that questions involving prime factors and long multiplication could ever have been thought to entail a measure of intelligence. If all other variables were accounted for, then it is just possible that such questions might have had a bearing on intelligence, but as a straightforward measure of inherent ability; never in a million years. For instance, if we had two children who had been given precisely similar teaching and both came from exactly the same sort of home with identical levels of parental involvement, then the fact that one readily grasped the principle of long multiplication, while the other was a little slower, might tell us something.

In practice, of course, it would never be possible to compensate for the million and one varying circumstances in the lives of the two children. The most likely thing that such a question would be able to tell you was who had been to a good school and who had not. In all probability, questions like this would tell you nothing useful about the child; merely give clues as to the nature of his or her environment.

> I was in the A stream all the way through primary school and by the time I reached 4A and the 11-plus was looming, it was pretty plain that our teacher expected most of us to pass it and go to grammar school. There's a lot of talk these days about league tables and 'teaching to the test', but that's nothing new. We knew that our teacher would feel that we had let her down if we failed. She had a reputation for having very high rates of success in getting her pupils through the 11-plus and that was why she stayed in charge of 4A. The other teachers at the school moved around a bit, maybe teaching the first years one year and 3B the next. Miss Cook, though, just stayed in 4A, making sure as many as possible passed their 11-plus. I heard later that it was a matter of pride for the head that his school got more children into the grammar than any other for miles around. Miss Cook worked us relentlessly as the 11-plus came closer. There was no nonsense here about this just being intended to measure intelligence; she told us plainly that the harder we worked that term, the more chance we had of getting through it. (Peter A. Barker)

This just goes to show that even those working within the education system had no illusions about the 11-plus, realising that it was just another academic examination which they could get children to pass by making them work hard. No pretence at all about this being a measure of anything other than good education.

We are beginning to get some idea of what this examination was really measuring and it was certainly something a little more complex than raw intelligence. The following is another sample question from the 11-plus exam:

The following incidents occur in well-known books you may have read:

i.   Tom comes down the wrong chimney
ii.   Jim discovers the chart of Treasure Island
iii.   Crusoe discovers a footprint in the sand
iv.   Jo visits Laurie for the first time
v.   Alice drinks from the little bottle
vi.   Black Beauty hears the hounds

Describe briefly two of these incidents.

Which sort of child would be best able to answer questions which centre on the plots of *Little Women* and *The Water Babies* – one from a bookish home attending a good primary school or one who came from a deprived home and was in the C stream of an under-performing school? A woman who took the exam in 1956 gives her own impressions:

My parents took it for granted that I would pass the 11-plus. They had been sold the idea that it was some sort of IQ test and so were content to let me sit it without any sort of preparation. I was bright enough and they just told me to do my best. The trouble was that we hadn't covered a lot of the maths which was in the test. I had no idea what prime factors were; much less how one would find them. Then there was a question about various classical composers. I hadn't heard of any of them, except vaguely Beethoven. I certainly was not capable of writing anything even remotely sensible about any of them. I was almost in tears by the end of it. I failed. (Dorothy Dobson)

I was the only one in the family who passed the 11-plus. My brothers were dead keen on football, but I had asthma and so didn't care so much for running round out of doors. Because of this, I used to read a lot and became pretty bookish. My two brothers were just as good as I was at maths, but their general knowledge was pretty poor and they hardly ever read anything unless they were made to at school. We took the exam at intervals of about eighteen months and later talked of what we found easy and what was tricky. We all did well enough at maths, but they fell down badly on the questions about general knowledge. None of this was anything to do with their intelligence, or mine. It simply meant that I had read more and so knew more of the things that the questions asked about. (Glynn Mitchell)

If the children who passed the 11-plus were not being selected on the basis of their intelligence, then what were the factors which caused one child to gain a grammar school place and another to end up in a secondary modern? The immediate and direct beneficiaries of the new examination were, in many cases, the same children who would already have been going to the grammar schools before they had thrown open their doors and stopped charging fees.

> I will never forget my father's reaction when he heard about grammar schools being made free and the new examination which children would have to sit in future to get places in them. I was thirteen at the time and at grammar school. My brother was two years above me, and my father was always moaning about how much the fees cost him. Now my nine-year-old brother would be able to go for nothing and there would be no more fees for both me and my brother. My father was quite literally rubbing his hands together with delight. The new system was going to save him a fortune. (David P. Taylor)

It is worth noting that throughout the late 1940s and '50s, half of the children attending grammar schools were from middle-class families. This was wholly disproportionate to the size of the middle class at that time and suggested that they were taking up more than their fair share of places at grammar schools. Among the working-class children at grammar schools, very few came from the families of unskilled or semi-skilled workers. In secondary moderns only 20 per cent of the children were from middle-class families.

When the 11-plus was first introduced, the idea was for the most intelligent 20 per cent of schoolchildren to go on to study at grammar schools. However, it quickly became obvious that this was not the case. For one thing, there was a very wide regional difference in the number of children passing the 11-plus. In the rural county of Westmoreland, 40 per cent of children passed the 11-plus, but seventy miles away in Sunderland only 10 per cent were getting to grammar schools – in some districts, as few as 2 per cent of the children were passing the 11-plus and going to grammar schools. Could it really be true that there were four times the amount of intellectual children in the Lake District as there were in a city in the North East?

> We knew that hardly anybody in our street and the ones nearby would be passing the 11-plus. We also knew that across the city in the 'nice' areas, a lot of the kids there would be going to grammar school. The few boys who lived near us and went to grammar school stuck out like sore thumbs. We all wore anything we wanted for school and they had nice blazers and caps. There were other parts of the city where it was just the opposite; loads of kids in grammar school uniform and only a few dressed casually and going to the secondary modern. I don't think we ever put it into words, but we somehow knew that posh kids went to grammar school and people like us went to secondary moderns. (Harry R. Smith)

> I grew up in what you might call a 'leafy suburb'. At half four in the afternoon, it was nearly all grammar school pupils that you saw coming home for tea. Hardly any of the teenagers in that area went to the secondary modern. There was a kind of feeling that children in that district would be going to the grammar school. Most of our older brothers and sisters went there and it was what was expected of you. It would have caused a great shock in our house if I had failed my 11-plus and had to go to the secondary modern. (Peter A. Barker)

Of course, if the 11-plus really was distinguishing the varying degrees of children's intellect, then there should have been no preconceived notions of which school you would attend depending on where you lived. So why was there such a dramatic difference in the percentage of children passing the exam in relation to geographical location and the social class of parents?

> I enjoyed the 11-plus. I suppose that I liked showing off when I was that age and the 11-plus gave me the chance to do so. One question wanted me to write a few sentences about *Black Beauty* and *Treasure Island*, which happened to be two of my favourite books. Then I had to write a bit about St Paul's Cathedral. Well, I'd been there a few times with my parents, so that was all right as well. I couldn't then – and still can't to this day – see how this was going to tell anybody anything about how intelligent I was, but there it was. I passed. (Keith J. Ballard)

My parents had always encouraged me to write down any stories
which I made up. When I was eight, I wrote this long saga about a dog
called Jock. I illustrated it with drawings and my parents bound the
whole thing so that it looked like a real book. Of course, this sort of
respect for what I was doing made me want to write all the more and
so I produced a series of short books with their help; it was more or less
my hobby for a couple of years. It was when I took the 11-plus that I
realised just how helpful all this had been as I was growing up. I had
to write a composition beginning: 'Imagine yourself on a long journey
in an aeroplane. Your engine fails and you have to land on a desert
island. Describe the island and tell what happens to you there.' This
was just the sort of thing that I had had so much practice at. I started
writing at once, but I was also aware that some of those around me
were staring despairingly into space; obviously with not the least idea
how to go about it. (Peter A. Barker)

If some children were left with a sense of failure after the results of
their 11-plus became known, there were others who suffered from their
success. At least those from working-class districts had the consolation of
knowing that they were not alone and that they would have a ready-made
circle of friends when they began at the secondary modern. For some of
the working-class children who did make it to grammar school, things
could be pretty lonely.

I was the only boy from round where I lived to get into the grammar
school. To be honest, I think a lot of my mates didn't even try. We had
a bit of contempt for the boys wearing blazers and caps when we saw
them and it wasn't unknown for grammar school boys to be roughed
up. I have always done my best at anything I put my hand to though
and the 11-plus was no exception. My parents were thrilled, it gave
them something to boast about to the neighbours, but within a few
days of the start of term, I knew that I would have been happier at
the secondary modern. Most of the boys in my class were what you
might call posh. The few other working-class kids were from different
areas from me and so I had no more in common with them than the
stuck-up boys. The teachers didn't really like boys like us either. This
was 1948 and until three or four years previously, this had been a
very old and respectable private school. Now they were being forced

by the government to take any old riff raff! I hated my time there and left as soon as I could when I was fifteen. (Glynn Mitchell)

From the moment I started at the grammar, I didn't seem to belong anywhere at all. My working-class accent marked me out at school and when I tried to change it and talk 'posh', I found my family and friends looking at me askance. A lot of the grammar school boys looked down on me and the boys I had known who had gone to the secondary modern, now looked upon me as a snob who thought he was too good for them. I just couldn't win. (Paul M. Richardson)

Not only could some children find themselves becoming estranged from their previous friends, this could also happen within families. Just because one sibling passed that all-important examination, it was no guarantee that his brothers and sisters would also get through it.

I am seventy-one, my brother is in his late sixties and I have a sister who is two years older than me. It hardly seems possible, but the after effects of passing my 11-plus sixty years ago still linger on. My sister failed it, although everybody thought she would pass and, later on, my brother also failed. I passed and this created tension between us which had definitely not been there before. For one thing, to my parents I now became 'the clever one'. Jane had good looks and my brother was practical and good with his hands, but I was always the one with the brains. It was such nonsense, I wasn't at all any more intelligent than my brother and sister, but there it was. My mum was always telling them that they had to let me study in peace, because it was more important for me to do my homework than it was for them. We have never talked about it since, but it has always been there, a kind of low level, festering grudge. I am sure that had we all gone to the same school, it would not be there. The 11-plus actually soured my relations with my family. (Josephine A. Wilson)

I became, overnight, 'the bright one'. From the day she failed her 11-plus, my sister became 'the pretty one'. It was so horribly depressing, because as a teenage girl I would rather have been thought of as 'the pretty one'. Those ridiculous labels became established as a kind of family myth, which was accepted by all our relations. If I said anything,

my aunts would say, 'Eh, listen to what she says, now. She's the one
with the brains.' It was this that the 11-plus did, defined people at a
very early age and told them what sort of people they were and would
probably be for the rest of their lives. Even now, my sister still defers
to my opinions because I am supposed to be 'the bright one'. Awful.
(Ellen T. Cade)

The anticipation of results day could be excruciating. The news was
delivered in different ways in different schools. Sometimes it was in
the form of a letter sent to the child's parents. This at least meant that
any upset could be endured privately with the family. In other schools
though, the news was given to the children by their teacher. Sometimes
this was done discretely; on other occasions in a spectacularly insensitive
fashion by means of an announcement during assembly, in front of the
whole school.

Almost unbelievably, the headmaster revealed the results of the
11-plus during a special assembly. This was done in the worst possible
way, by calling up to the stage those of us who had passed and shaking
our hands. Those who had failed only knew about it because they were
not called up to be congratulated. (Lillian O. Drake)

Some schools handled things a little better.

One morning, a message was sent to our class that the head would
like to see Mary Jones. Being sent to the head was normally a matter
of great anxiety; it only happened when you were in terrible trouble.
Mary went out looking terrified, but returned radiant. She said that
the head now wished to see Jack Smith. Over half the class were sent
for in this way and it was only at playtime that we discovered that
these children had been told that they had passed the 11-plus and
would accordingly be going to grammar school. Nothing was said to
the rest of us, but we deduced correctly that this must mean that we
would be staying on at this school and moving up into the secondary
modern. (Ronald G. Feeney)

The psychological pressure placed upon young children by all this could
be tremendous. It did not matter so much in schools where few children

were expected to pass anyway and nobody much cared, but in classes full of children from ambitious, middle-class homes a lot was riding on the results of this one examination.

> As results day approached, I became terribly anxious. I couldn't eat and lay awake at night worrying about what would happen if I had failed. I knew that it would mean that not only would I have let down my parents, but that my life would also be ruined; it was that obvious, at least in my mind. For my parents, everything in my life had been leading up to this moment. If I passed, then grammar school, sixth form and perhaps even university beckoned. If not, then I would end up being a butcher's boy, which was my father's favourite example of the only sort of career open to those who fetched up in secondary moderns. Fortunately, I passed. (Peter A. Barker)

> If it hadn't been for my parents, I don't think that I would fully have realised the supreme importance of the 11-plus. They paid for a teacher to coach me for weeks beforehand, and when my father got in from work on the day that I had taken it, he cross-examined me closely about the questions and how I had answered them. There was an air of suppressed, feverish tension in the house until we heard that I had actually passed. This was all my parents; the school itself did not make a particular fuss about the thing. (Keith J. Ballard)

It seems, in retrospect, incredible that it took twenty years for those in authority to see its disadvantages. That a child's entire future could be decided in the course of a few hours at the age of ten or eleven seems to us now a patently bad idea. Coaching could effect a dramatic improvement in scores of tests like the 11-plus and this coaching was far more likely to be offered to children of middle-class families; a doctor in the London borough of Richmond would be more likely to have the money and connections to arrange such coaching than would a miner in South Wales.

> I failed my 11-plus in 1949, but over the next couple of years I more or less figured out what the trick had been. I passed the 13-plus and transferred from the secondary modern to the grammar. After staying on in the sixth, I went to university and studied psychology.

Cyril Burt was still hugely influential during the 1950s, but there were already rumours about his work. One of my professors was very scathing about him and showed us the correlations that Burt was claiming about inherited intelligence. He knew and persuaded us that they could not possibly be right. In the 1970s, when it all came out, I felt a kind of grim satisfaction about the whole thing. I had known for years that I didn't fail my 11-plus because I was thick, but to find that the exam had been based on the work of such a crook was still pretty shocking. The funny thing is, you still hear people wishing that the 11-plus could be brought back, as though the 1950s were something marvellous for ordinary children as far as education goes. (Dorothy Dobson)

Whatever had earlier been claimed, the examination itself had little to do with intelligence and everything to do with previous schooling and education.

As if all this were not bad enough, the outcomes could be dramatically altered by something as simple and unpredictable as a bad cold on the day of sitting the tests. With the number of those able to pass being strictly limited by the number of places available at local grammar schools, competition could be ferocious. A couple of points could mean the difference between passing and failing. In fact, the child's state of health on the day could cause a variation of seventeen points in the final score. Children were being denied a place at grammar school and the chance to acquire qualifications and go on to university, simply because they happened to have a cold when they were ten years old!

In reality, the path to either a grammar or secondary modern school started long before the taking of the 11-plus. The type of school attended from the age of eleven in particular told you all you really needed to know about a child's future prospects. This was the case before the Second World War and it was still pretty much the case throughout the 1940s and '50s. If anything, it became possible even earlier in a child's life to predict the probable educational outcomes and, therefore, the likely course of their adult life. Before the war, one could see at eleven whether or not a child was going to transfer to a secondary school and so take the School Certificate. By the late 1940s, one could usually tell by the age of seven if a child would be taking examinations or leaving school without any qualifications at the age of fifteen.

Once the results of the 11-plus had been received, children knew whether they would be attending a secondary modern or a grammar school the following September – at least three quarters of children went to secondary moderns.

Secondary Moderns

When it came to secondary education, life continued pretty much as before in the grammar schools. True, they no longer charged fees and the proportion of scholarship pupils rose from 25 per cent to 100 per cent, but the numbers of pupils did not increase. Their existing buildings and staff were quite adequate for the new system. This was not at all the case with the new secondary modern schools. Here was an entirely new type of school, which would require new staff, new methods, new buildings and new furniture.

Before we go any further, it is worth considering the implications of the raising of the school leaving age from fourteen to fifteen and just why there was such opposition to the idea from all sides; not least the children and their families affected by this move. Only the secondary moderns were affected. The existing grammar schools were already geared to their pupils staying on until they were sixteen or eighteen.

Britain was rebuilding after six years of war. The Blitz had destroyed many homes; industry was getting into the swing of peacetime production; everywhere there was need for workers. Most of the jobs entailed physical strength rather than intellectual ability. Men were needed to carry loads in the docks, dig ditches on farms and work on building sites. These were the days when it was possible for a school leaver to walk into a factory or building site in the morning and to be working by lunchtime.

At the time, many thought that keeping children in school up to the age of fifteen to be pretty pointless.

We were just waiting for the day when we could leave. Some left before their fifteenth birthday and at first, nobody bothered much. In fact, for a few months it looked as though we would be able to carry on leaving at fourteen and nobody would do much about it. All good things come to an end though and one day the truancy officer began touring local building sites and tracking down all the fourteen-year-olds and then threatening to prosecute their parents. I can't tell you how much we wanted to get out of school and start earning. (Gregory Parker)

There was no money available at first to build any new schools and so the elementary schools had to be adapted and converted into secondary schools. It is one thing to pass a law, but one cannot alter facts of life. The truth is that the system of elementary schools continued in many parts of the country for ten or twelve years after the passing of the 1944 Education Act. The government and local authorities might be able to insist that the children did not leave until they were fifteen, but without huge sums of money, there was little they could do about the school buildings themselves and it was this which meant that things carried on more or less as usual for years after the end of the war.

I turned eleven in 1946 and went to the new secondary modern. I say new; it was really the Jubilee Street Elementary. It carried on being called that locally for the next ten years or so. They might have changed the sign outside and introduced a new exam, but it didn't make any real difference to how things worked. There had already been a scholarship exam before the war, which nobody passed where I lived. Again, they called it something different now, but the result was the same, none of the kids near where I lived passed it. We just carried on going to Jubilee Street until we were fourteen. Well, I say fourteen, but of course the year after I started there, they put up the leaving age. There didn't seem to be any sense in this, it was just meddling by the government. (Lorna Gavin)

Most state schools at that time were old Victorian board schools. These varied from poky little one-room village schools to vast buildings tricked out to look like eighteenth-century mansions. This type of building, more commonly found in cities, was perfectly adapted for the new role of secondary school. However, there was still the necessity to find space for another year's worth of pupils. The solution for this was the Hutting Operation for the Raising of the School leaving Age; HORSA for short. This entailed installing prefabricated concrete huts in playgrounds and on playing fields by the side of the local elementary school.

> Some of our lessons were held in the new concrete huts which sprang up like mushrooms from about 1947 onwards. I remember them being built. They arrived like flat-pack furniture, pre-cast concrete walls and corrugated, asbestos roofs. The windows were made of galvanised iron. Six of these things, the HORSA huts, were set up next to the main school building and they were used as extra classrooms. There was a very makeshift feel about them, they reminded me a bit of the old wartime Nissen huts or Anderson shelters. (Harry R. Smith)

> Even as a twelve year old in the early 1950s, I could sense that there was something sub-standard about the secondary modern which I was attending, at least compared to the grammar school down the road. The grammar school was a seventeenth-century building which looked like an ancient university. Our secondary modern was a Victorian school with the infants on the ground the floor. Half the playground had been given over to pre-fabricated huts in which we had some of our lessons. There was no heating in them and the roofs were not completely waterproof. During heavy rain, drips of water came through. It was like being taught in an old garage! (Ronald G. Feeney)

The HORSA huts gave the appearance of an army base or refugee camp to many of the newly established secondary moderns. The aim of the 1944 Education Act might well have been to introduce greater equality into education, but the premises told a different story.

The need for new school buildings was urgent and the HORSA huts were only a temporary measure. However, incredible as it may seem, some HORSA huts are still in use to this day. Gradually, the huts stopped being used as classrooms and were converted to serve other purposes. They became kitchens, lavatory blocks, woodwork rooms and laboratories. These temporary structures, thrown up in a hurry to deal with a pressing need, lasted so long that an extraordinary situation arose when it was finally decided to get rid of them. Because many of them were built before 1 July 1948, Listed Building Consent is needed for demolition or even any alterations. These prefabs, with asbestos roofs and cheap metal windows, now enjoy the same protected status as stately homes dating back to the Elizabethan era.

Apart from this, an observer would have been hard-pressed to spot much difference between life in many secondary modern schools and their previous incarnations as elementary schools.

> My brother passed his 11-plus and went to grammar school, while I was at the secondary modern. This gives me a pretty good insight into the differences between the two kinds of school. There was only eighteen months between us and we used to compare notes to see who was doing what. For instance, at his school, they were learning about famous artists and painting in watercolours. We did technical drawing, perspective views of book-cases and clocks. One big difference was that we were doing a lot of stuff like woodwork and metal work, but they didn't do anything like that at the grammar. Our maths was designed to be useful to us; working out the change from £10 or how many planks would be needed to cover a floor. At the same age, he was doing calculus. (John B. Fleming)

> By and large, as long as we didn't make trouble or anything, the teachers seemed happy for us to do what we pleased. There were some who wanted to learn and they used to concentrate on them and leave the rest of us alone. We had an allotment where we were supposed to be learning about gardening and so a bunch of us would just sit behind the shed smoking. As long as we were quiet, nobody seemed bothered. (Brenda Jacobs)

This, of course, was precisely what well-meaning people like Ellen Wilkinson had hoped to avoid; schools just being used as warehouses and waiting rooms for young people before they started work. If the boys at the secondary moderns were being prepared for a life of work in a factory, the likely destiny of the girls was also clearly signposted and could be divined by the sort of things that they were being taught there.

> We used to do a lot of what used to be called Mothercraft but is now called Domestic Science. Basically, this meant housework. Cooking, cleaning and looking after a baby, that sort of thing. We had a special

building in the grounds where we used to go for this. It was more or less taken for granted that we were all going to end up as housewives. Of course, we might have a little job for a while before that and so they also taught us shorthand and typing. (Catherine E. Kingsley)

Of course, not all secondary modern schools were like this; some expected a lot more. A few tried to copy the grammar schools as closely as possible. Some secondary moderns didn't have a uniform and the pupils dressed how they pleased. Others insisted on uniforms as strict as at any grammar school. There was a problem with this sort of school though, however well meaning it was and however great the ambitions for children who had failed the 11-plus. This related to the taking of examinations.

At grammar schools, the pupils took first the School Certificate and later the General Certificate of Education in the year that they became sixteen. One had to take a selection of six subjects for the School Certificate, including English and Mathematics. Typically, these might include History, Science, French, Geography and so on. At the secondary moderns, these subjects were often not taught at all. This, combined with the fact that they left at fifteen rather than sixteen, meant that qualifications like the School Certificate or GCEs were not open to pupils at a secondary modern. From 1965 onwards, secondary modern pupils could sit examinations for the Certificate of Secondary Education, otherwise known as the CSE, but for twenty years it was quite literally impossible for most of those who failed the 11-plus to take examinations at school, however bright they were. And some of them were certainly bright enough to take GCEs, as we shall see shortly.

> I left school with nothing at all; absolutely nothing to show for the four years that I had spent in the secondary modern. Even a routine clerical job in a bank or the civil service had minimum requirements of GCE in English and maths. That meant that hardly anybody from a secondary modern could even apply to work in an office. I went to evening classes at the local technical college after I left school and took my GCEs that way. Most of the boys I was at school with didn't bother though. (Harry R. Smith)

> I knew that I was just as capable of taking GCEs as the friends who had passed their 11-plus, but there was nothing to be done about it. This

was before the CSE, and once you had been sent to one school or the other that was it. It was either GCEs at the grammar or nothing at all at the secondary modern. (Brenda Jacobs)

Why didn't secondary moderns start offering the chance to sit the GCEs to their pupils? In the late 1940s it would have been almost impossible to do so, as it would have required extra staff to teach the children to that level, and to cope with all the young people who would not now be leaving school at fourteen. One of the ways in which this was at least attempted to be remedied was by engaging new teachers, some of whom were not properly trained. Many had been soldiers hastily retrained after their demobilisation. The quality of these new teachers was not at the same levels as those to be found in old, established grammar schools. After all, nothing much was being expected of these new teachers. If they could somehow control a roomful of rowdy fifteen-year-olds and prevent them from murdering each other, that would be quite sufficient. The new teachers at the secondary moderns might have been able to keep order, but being able to steer their pupils through the intricacies of studying for and taking GCEs was likely to be beyond most of them.

> Actually, I enjoyed my time at the secondary modern. At juniors we were always being chivvied about and made to work in preparation for the dreaded 11-plus. Once we had failed it though, the pressure was off. We weren't going to be taking O levels or anything like that and so we could just take it easy. At least, that's how I saw it. (Catherine E. Kingsley)

> I had never had much use for book learning and so the secondary modern came as a pleasant change. Instead of being made to learn things like long division and the exports of Australia, we were doing real things like typing and learning how to cook. I thought then, and still think sixty years later, that this was more use to most of us than learning algebra and Latin would have been. (Brenda Jacobs)

There was a severe lack of career or life choice for a girl during this time, and most young women leaving school, whether from a secondary modern or grammar school, would ultimately end up running homes and looking after children.

A girl from a grammar school might, if she wished, decide to go on to university or embark upon a professional career. For the girl leaving the secondary modern at the age of fifteen with no qualifications, such choices were not open to her. She could only look forward to a routine job in a factory or shop, followed by life as a housewife.

In the 1950s, some teachers began to notice that youngsters who took a transfer examination and moved from the secondary modern to the grammar school were not only able keep up, but sometimes actually overtook those who had already been at the grammar school for a couple of years. Some secondary moderns managed to obtain permission and funding from their Local Education Authorities to enter pupils for GCEs. The secondary modern pupils proved no less able to acquire the qualifications for which children enrolled at grammar school were being prepared. It began to dawn on many in the educational world as the 1950s drew on, that there was something amiss with the 1944 Education Act.

> Our school, which was a secondary modern, tried the experiment of letting some of the brighter kids stay on and sit GCE levels. It didn't take long for them to realise that there was something fishy going on, because our results were almost as good as those at the grammar school. We didn't get as many, but that was only because we weren't entered for as many. For maths and English, the results were brilliant. You could almost see the cogs turning in the teachers' heads, as they realised that we were just as capable as the kids in the grammar down the road! (Harry R. Smith)

Some of the first secondary moderns to be built were pretty grim, but others were examples of a new sort of school; quite different from both the grammar schools and the Victorian elementary schools in which most secondary moderns had been accommodated. From the mid-1950s, new secondary schools began to be opened – some secondary modern and some comprehensive – which looked nothing like the existing schools. These were exciting, original buildings, offering facilities better than even the grammars.

Considering that between 75 and 80 per cent of young people went to secondary moderns, rather than private schools or grammars, the secondary modern school has left remarkably little imprint upon the cultural history of the times. Books about children at boarding schools were still being churned out, along with William at his grammar school, but, with one or two exceptions, the secondary modern didn't feature in any fiction; either for children or for adults.

There were one or two books about the experience of teaching in such schools during the 1950s. Perhaps the most famous of these is *To Sir with Love*, an autobiographical novel by E.R. Braithwaite, a Guyanan teacher. It is a thinly disguised account of Braithwaite's time as a teacher at a secondary modern in east London.

> I remember seeing *To Sir with Love* when it came out at the cinema and thinking that that was exactly what my school had been like; the awkward pupils, the bloody-mindedness; just everything. Later on, I read the book and it all rang very true. This is the only book that I have ever seen that even mentions secondary moderns though. (Harry R. Smith)

It is interesting that it took somebody from another country to write the definitive book about secondary moderns in the 1950s. Perhaps Braithwaite was not aware of the British convention, whereby only boarding schools must be generally written about in memoirs!

There was a constant feeling, which lasted well into the 1950s, that both government and local authorities begrudged the money which they were compelled to spend upon secondary moderns. In the early 1950s, a plan emerged in the Cabinet that the school leaving age should be lowered back to fourteen. It was believed that this would have many advantages; firstly, it would free up thousands of young people to join the workforce. These youngsters would then start contributing to the economy by means of taxes, and their spending power would also give a boost to manufacturing. Secondly, it would save a fortune on salaries for teachers and the need for new buildings. With any luck, it might be possible to continue hobbling along with the old buildings, supplemented by the HORSA huts for another decade or two. Fortunately, this plan was never proceeded with.

> I was going mad in my last year at school. It all seemed so utterly pointless. I took a lot of time off and for a while I was working on the market. I don't think the head cared about those of us that hardly ever came in, but one day the inspectors visited and must have given him a right talking to, because a few of us got letters sent home threatening to take out parents to court if we didn't come to school every day.

I carried on working one day a week in the market and every so often
my teacher would tell me that I had to come in to school every day for
a bit or we'd all be in trouble. There were a few others in my class doing
the same kind of thing. (Gregory Parker)

Local authorities might be compelled to run secondary modern schools
and insist that children attended them up to the age of fifteen, but they
took care to spend as little as possible on them. Apart from buildings,
which were still being done on the cheap with the prefabricated HORSA
huts, the other big expense for schools was of course the teachers' salaries.

The staffing analogue to the HORSA was the Emergency Training
Scheme for Teachers, which ran from 1945 to 1951. This produced over
35,000 new teachers, each of whom received just one year's training, and
many of whom lacked qualifications. There were actually no educational
prerequisites for being given a place on the new training scheme, they were
selected mainly on their personalities and perceived ability to cope with a
large classroom full of noisy children. Almost all worked in either primary
schools or secondary moderns. It was emphasised by the Ministry of
Education that these new teachers were not to be seen as being in any way
inferior to those who had gone through the traditional routes and perhaps
had degrees. The scheme was launched in 1943, two years before the war
ended, and even then it was perhaps assumed that most of these hastily
trained teachers would be not be going to work in grammar schools.

I was at school from 1946 to 1956, ending at a secondary modern.
We had some very peculiar teachers. One man was half blind and also
suffered from shell shock. He used to shout and rave if we made a noise
and so the trick of it was that we just talked quietly and played games
without making a noise. I don't believe that he actually taught us
anything, but we were so scared of him that we made an effort to keep
quiet. At the last year in juniors, we had a teacher who could have
been no more than eighteen or nineteen. She was a lovely, gentle girl,
but quite unable to control us. We made her life a misery and more
than once reduced her to tears. In secondary school, the teachers we
feared most were the ex-army types. They had been used to discipline
themselves and knew how to maintain order. Again, I have to say that
they weren't very good at teaching us anything. They made good PE
teachers though. (Harry R. Smith)

I don't think that some of the teachers we had in the years just after the war would be acceptable today. One fellow, an ex-soldier, used a walking stick and if he was very annoyed, he would lash out with it at the nearest boy. The ones who had been in the army usually knew how to keep order. I have an idea that some of them weren't very well educated themselves though and how they became teachers, I have no idea. (Ronald G. Feeney)

Inevitably, taking on tens of thousands of new and mostly unqualified teachers in this way was going to create some difficulties.

Several teachers at our secondary school just vanished and we never learned what had happened. There were rumours that one had been taken off to a mental hospital and that another had been arrested, but nobody knew for sure. There was a very high turnover of staff, with some teachers only staying for a term or so. This would have been around 1949. The teachers seemed to be either fairly old types who had been in teaching for many years or young men out of the army. They didn't say anything to us directly, but I have an idea that the older teachers didn't really approve of a lot of the newly qualified men who were being drafted in. (Sheila Fawcett)

There was a lot of resentment on the part of many of the young people forced to stay on at school after the raising of the school leaving age and to prevent these young people from becoming disaffected, novel approaches were sometimes needed. The newly trained and poorly qualified teachers who found their way to the secondary moderns were not always a bad thing.

The third and fourth year at our secondary modern were notoriously hard to teach. We took something of a pride in this, the idea that we were un-teachable. The only ones who ever managed to do anything with us were the younger men who had just been demobilised and rushed through a teacher training course. They weren't soft, far from it, but some of these men were prepared to treat us as adults and we responded to that. A few of them were very working class themselves and so there was no point in us taking the piss out of the way they spoke behind their backs. They were just like us. The head didn't really care what they did with us as long as we didn't riot or burn down the school and so one or two got permission to take us out and about, instead of keeping us cooped up in the classroom. We went to visit factories, a farm and a couple of garages. I think the idea was to let us see a few workplaces. I have no idea how it was all arranged. Normally, we were an utter nightmare when being taken out anywhere, but for these expeditions, we behaved impeccably. (Brenda Jacobs)

One of the great things about being at a secondary modern was the freedom to follow your own interests. We weren't going to be taking exams or anything and so there was a lot of leeway in what we did. Some of the teachers were fantastic for this. One had an old car that he brought in and taught us how to change the tyres, check the oil, all sorts of things. He was an army man and he had a real way with the boys. We would have done anything for that man and the head was just happy to see us actually doing something other than make trouble. We tuned the car's engine and he gave us lessons, let us drive the thing round the playing field. It was an absolute nightmare from a health and safety viewpoint, but we learned more with that one teacher than the rest put together. (Harry R. Smith)

In primary schools, grammars and secondary moderns, there was far more scope at this time for the unconventional person – the maverick with apparently mad ideas. Teachers like the fictional Jean Brodie, from the novel *The Prime of Miss Jean Brodie*, were not unusual in the years following the war. Today, teacher training is standardised and all members of staff must follow the same procedures, teach the same syllabus and abide by the same rules. The situation was more easy-going in the 1950s, with some men and women who would now be thought most unsuitable to be working in a classroom.

We had one teacher that used to smoke during lessons. He would stand by the window to do it, but the smell of those full-strength Capstans was still pretty overpowering. You just can't imagine that today; a teacher having a fag during a lesson. We had another bloke who went to the pub at lunchtime and used to come back a bit worse for wear. He would set us the work and then sit down and like as not have a snooze. They had trouble getting teachers in some of the rougher secondary moderns and so they really had to take who they could get. (Catherine E. Kingsley)

There were some real characters among the staff at my grammar school – older women who had never married and regarded the girls almost as being their children. We used to go back to visit after leaving and these teachers were always pleased to hear how we were getting on. Until recently I was a governor at my old school and I can't help noticing that individuality seems to have gone from teachers these days. They all have the same outlook, very much wedded to a particular line and obsessed with the curriculum. They don't seem to be concerned with the girls as rounded individuals, only with how many GCSEs and A Levels they can push them through. That's the only measure now of schools, of course; the numbers of qualifications gained.

Grammar Schools

One of the main aims of the 1944 Education Act was to ensure that every child in the country had free access to secondary education. The most desirable sort of secondary education was of course that provided in the grammar schools, often viewed as bastions of privilege, and before the Second World War were private. A quarter of their places were set aside for scholarship boys and girls. Although these places were supposedly available to children from all walks of life, the majority of the time they were given to slightly impoverished middle-class children. This was not at all what was supposed to be happening after the end of the war and it came as something of a surprise to many children from poorer backgrounds who had gained places at the local grammar school via the 11-plus, to discover just how few children at these places were taken by others like them.

I was one of only two – I suppose the word I am looking for is 'ordinary' – boys in the first year when I started at the grammar school in 1951. I definitely felt left out. All the other boys seemed to fit together. I don't mean that they knew each other, but they knew how to hold their knives and forks properly, to say 'Sorry' rather than 'Pardon', and use words like 'lavatory' instead of 'toilet'. All this sounds really unimportant now, but at the time it meant a lot. There would be sly smiles and exchanged glances when I used certain expressions or didn't know about some social convention. The teachers too didn't seem to take kindly to boys like me. I think that some of them wished that the grammar was still private and regretted having the wrong sort of pupils allowed in. (Paul M. Richardson)

If they gained a place at the grammar school, then it would be necessary to stay on until sixteen if they wished to sit GCEs. Many working-class children at grammar school, perhaps a quarter of them, did not do so. They left at fifteen and were in precisely the same position as a secondary modern pupil leaving school at the same age. Even those who did stay on until sixteen and sit examinations found that things did not go as well as they might have hoped.

> I was at grammar school and left with three GCEs. I thought that I was set up for a decent job, after all, friends who had gone to the secondary modern didn't have any GCEs at all. I soon found though that three GCEs weren't much use on the job market. The banks wanted five as the minimum, as did the council if you wanted a clerical job with them. The fact that you had been to the grammar and only managed to get three GCEs made it look to potential employers as though you were probably lazy or thick. I didn't realise at the time how important they would be. (Glynn Mitchell)

> I did take my GCEs, but I didn't know that some were more important than others. I had scripture and metalwork, but these didn't count really when you were totting them up. Although I had five, I still wasn't given a place in the sixth. (John B. Fleming)

One curious feature of many grammar schools at that time is the Combined Cadet Forces (CCF) which was established at so many. The grammars and independents had supplied the overwhelming majority of officers during the Second World War and there was no reason at all to suppose that this would not continue to be the case in the future. It had been like that for every war since Queen Victoria's reign and it seemed inevitable that this situation would endure for the foreseeable future. The way to ensure that those young men had the necessary qualities to become officer material was to give them a bit of practice before they even left school.

> Our grammar school, Ilford County High, had a range next to the school buildings. It was an old Nissen hut type thing, made of corrugated iron. I was in the cadets and we used to shoot there after school. Next to the head's office was the armoury. This was a locked

walk-in cupboard which contained an absolutely unbelievable array
of firearms. Not just rifles – both .303 and .22, – but also sub-machine
guns, an entire rack of old Sten guns and also a few Brens, not to
mention the dozens of .38 revolvers. (Paul M. Richardson)

It must of course be borne in mind that it was almost twenty years after
the end of the war that conscription, also known as National Service,
was abolished. As a matter of course, all the boys at school, with very few
exceptions, would be serving in the armed forces within a year or two of
leaving school. In a way, it made perfect sense for them to become famil-
iarised with firearms while they were young. It was possible to join the
CCF and start handling and firing guns at the age of thirteen.

I joined the CCF as soon as I could. We had our own hut in the school
grounds and did drill and so on; also a lot of shooting. All sorts of
weapons, from .22 target rifles to fully automatic stuff; light machine
guns like Brens. The army recruiting people kept a close eye on our
school, which was a grammar. Their line was that since we would all
have to go into the army anyway for National Service, why didn't we
think about going in as officers, perhaps even making a career of it?
(Keith J. Ballard)

It is perhaps significant that CCFs of this type were to be found only in
grammar and independent schools. There do not seem to have been any
in secondary modern schools. Perhaps it was assumed that the boys
leaving school at fifteen from the secondary moderns would invariably
end up as privates when they were called up at the age of eighteen. The
officers would be drawn from the ranks of the upper and middle classes,
who would of course be unlikely to be found in secondary modern
schools. This is just one more example of the way in which the different
schools channelled young people into different paths through life, with
quite different expectations.

Being at a grammar school was a very different experience in so
many different ways to that of being at a secondary modern. It must
be remembered that if secondary moderns suffered from inferiority
complexes because they were not grammar schools, so too did grammar
schools feel second rate because they were not public schools. A lot of
the traditions and customs found at grammar schools at this time were

not centuries old, as they were in places such as Eton, but had been introduced in the late nineteenth century in a self-conscious effort to imitate the public schools.

> I failed the 11-plus and went to the secondary modern. Then, when I was thirteen, I passed the transfer exam and moved to the grammar school. Because of this, I have seen both systems in practice. The secondary modern was just that; modern. The grammar school though seemed to go out of its way to have special rules and customs to mark itself apart from ordinary schools. To give one example, most of the masters wore gowns. I forget the reason for this; I think maybe they were the ones with degrees. Also they were 'masters' and not teachers. There were things like short prayers in Latin that sounded as though they were something that had been preserved as a hallowed tradition. I found out later that this particular tradition was less than fifty years old. Some head had visited a public school and thought it sounded impressive, so he had simply imported it as a ready-made custom! (John B. Fleming)

> There was something horribly bogus about our grammar school. The masters in their gowns, the Latin motto, the school song; the whole works. This school was not some ancient and venerable institution; it had only been going for less than a hundred years. Nevertheless, they were desperate to make themselves appear as though they had a history dating back to the Tudors. I suppose you can't blame them. Until 1945, they were a fee-paying school and I guess that the parents wanted a bit of history and tradition for their money. They really laid it on thick at open days, with grace being said in Latin and extra little touches of that sort. (David P. Taylor)

There is no doubt that in addition to their usefulness in getting children the qualifications that they would need to get on, there was also a purely social cachet in having your children at a grammar school rather than a secondary modern. For many middle-class parents, it would have been regarded as very embarrassing to admit to your friends that little Johnny had failed his 11-plus and was at the local secondary modern! This would have been particularly so when the prevailing orthodoxy was in favour of the heritability of intelligence. If one's child failed the

11-plus, it must surely be because you didn't hand on the correct genetic inheritance; presumably because you were a little lacking yourself in the brain cells department.

> I clearly remember my mother's response when she found out that I had failed the 11-plus. Whatever will people think? Although we lived in a fairly down-at-heel area, my mother had been used to better things, or that at least was the impression she liked to give. She had been looking forward to having me wearing a blazer and cap; it would demonstrate to the neighbours, upon whom she looked down, that we didn't really belong in this street at all. It sounds mad, but there was a lot more feeling of class in those days. And then her son had let her down and proved to be no brighter than the rough boys next door. She cared a lot more than I did about my failure to get to the grammar school. (Ronald G. Feeney)

The grammar school cap symbolised so much; it represented learning, success, and, on top of all that, it indicated that the child's parents were the 'right sort'. Truly, there was a lot riding on the result of the 11-plus, even leaving aside any possible educational benefit.

> I knew even before I took the 11-plus that going to grammar school was the sort of thing that people like us did. I can't really explain any better than to say that it was taken as a given. There were little remarks about 'secondary modern boys' and not in a good way. I gained the impression that being a secondary modern boy was not what was expected of one. It was nothing at all to do with education mind; it was more about the way that people behaved. Secondary modern in my parents eyes equated with 'loutish and ill mannered'. Obviously, grammar school boys were the very antithesis of this and so that was what they wished me to be. At ten or eleven, I was not thinking in terms of taking O levels or A levels, it was just that I wanted to be a well-behaved young man and a credit to my parents and that was what grammar schools represented. (Peter A. Barker)

I don't think that my father ever really cottoned on to the fact that his old school had effectively been nationalised and now belonged to the local council. It was only a grammar school, founded in the nineteenth century, but he spoke of it as though it were Eton or Harrow. The thought that anybody at all could get into it now for nothing filled him with horror. After a few years though, under new management as it were, he gradually began to relax as he saw that exactly the same kind of boys were going there as had always been the case. Instead of spending their money on school fees, he and his friends were buying their way in by having their sons tutored at weekends and in the evenings. (Conrad Summerfield)

Families who could afford to pay for only some of their child's education, often tried to economise by creating a mix and match arrangement of private and state schools. For instance, if there was a fairly reasonable elementary school or village school nearby a child might be sent there up to the age of eleven, following which a private education would be paid for at a grammar school. This was primarily done because not all families could afford to have their child educated privately from the age of five to eighteen. This is not, of course, how the matter was represented to one's friends. Since elementary schools were mixed and also had female as well as male teachers, a mother might claim that her rough boy would benefit from having some feminine influence during his formative years and so they had decided to send him somewhere where he would be able to mix with girls.

We lived in a small town in Oxfordshire and my parents sent me to the village school until I was eleven. I mixed with all sorts of kids there and it was very good for me. The stated aim was so that I could be exposed to the softening influence of lady teachers and spending my time with girls as well as boys. If this had been the real reason, then it was a disastrous flop, because I gravitated quite naturally to the roughest boys in the school; the sons of labourers and farm workers. I became their companion and a member of the closest thing that a pre-war rural community had to a 'gang'. When I was eleven, I went to the grammar school as a fee-paying pupil. I only learned later that the whole business about the village school was really because my father couldn't afford to have me privately educated all the way from the age of five. (David P. Taylor)

When grammar schools became free to all parents, some of those who had previously been paying for their children to attend, switched tactics and decided to invest money in early private education instead. Sending a child to a good private school until the age of eleven would make it more likely that he or she would be able to pass the 11-plus and thus get into the grammar school. The private preparatory schools were, of course, all single sex.

I was sent in 1947 to a small private girls school. I spent five years there and then, after passing my 11-plus, I went to the local county high; the best grammar school in the city. I think that this worked out cheaper for my parents than the old method would have been. Before the war, they would have sent me to the local school and then paid for the grammar until I was eighteen. This would have entailed seven years of school fees, but that was now reduced to five. (Anon)

We only lived a couple of streets from the grammar school, but it didn't feel like our local secondary school. Most of the people living nearby expected their children to go to the secondary modern about a mile away. We used to see the boys arriving at the grammar school with their caps and blazers; hardly any of them lived nearby. This would have been in the late 1940s, say three or four years after the war ended. Of course, we knew that the new education system had opened up the grammar schools to everybody, but you wouldn't have known it to see how things worked out where we lived. The kids in our street were still going to the old elementary school and the boys from the posh suburbs were still travelling to the grammar school. There was no change that we could see. (Glynn Mitchell)

The Independent Sector

It is hard to judge whether private schools during the 1940s and '50s were more or less exclusive than is now the case. Accurate figures are not always possible to come by but of one thing we may be sure; those educated in such establishments were, just as today, a small minority. Perhaps less than one child in twenty was being taught at independent schools during this period.

I simply took being sent to private schools for granted when I was growing up. I was vaguely aware that there was a school about half a mile from where we lived, but I didn't know anybody who went there or indeed anything at all about it. I sometimes felt a little wistful, because the girls there seemed to have a good deal more life in them than those with whom I spent my own school days. We were discouraged from shouting, running, talking loudly, showing off or being in any way anything other than completely self-controlled. When we went anywhere outside school, we walked in twos, holding hands; a neat little crocodile of perfectly quiet and well-behaved young ladies of ten or eleven. Grown-ups were always delighted at the sight, but I would rather have been pelting down the road shouting across the street to my friends like any normal child of that age. (Anon)

Prep school, boarding of course, from eight, followed by Eton. During holidays, I was actively discouraged by my parents from making friends with any of the boys who lived locally. The emphasis was on being an adult; any sort of rowdy or childish behaviour was frowned upon, especially by my father. Even in the early 1950s, it was quite possible for a boy to grow up in a big city like London and never meet anybody of a different class. I only associated with the children of my parents' friends and they were all fairly well off as well. I certainly never played with any boys from the neighbourhood of our home; I honestly can't remember even speaking to any! (James R. Harker)

It could be said that at the back of many middle-class parents' minds was the fear that if their child spent too much time in the company of working-class children, he would pick up dreadful habits; ranging from dropping his aitches to stealing from shops; far safer if he was restricted to a better class of company. During the holidays they could be sent to stay with family members in out of the way places, thus preventing them from forming any unsuitable attachments which might flourish away from boarding school. In this way, it was perfectly feasible to ensure that a child from a wealthy or privileged home did not even meet a working-class child.

For less well off middle-class families, this was not always possible. Before the war, they not infrequently had to limit the private education for their child to a grammar school at the age of eleven. For the early years, many were obliged to rely upon state schools. This was the pattern before the Second World War and it is described perfectly in Richmal Crompton's *William* books. It will be recalled that in some of the earlier books, William is attending a 'village school' – presumably one of the all-age elementary schools. Later on, he is placed in a fee-paying grammar school. The chief disadvantage of this arrangement was that William, unlike the sons of the seriously wealthy, was able to meet and associate with some pretty unsuitable types. For his birthday, he asked his mother if he might invite the butcher's boy; an idea which his mother indignantly rejects out of hand. It was certain families of this sort who switched to private education in the late 1940s, when the practical consequences of Butler's Education Act were becoming apparent.

I was due to go to the grammar school in 1946, but my father changed his mind when the 11-plus was brought in and the places became open to all. At the time, he claimed that he was worried that the standards would slip if they let just anybody in. I am sure that those listening to him would have understood that he was really concerned that I might start mixing with the wrong crowd. It was only many years later that I learned the real reason for his having abandoned the grammar school scheme for his only son. I was not flattered to find out that he thought that I was not bright enough to pass the 11-plus and so, rather than risk everybody hearing that his son was an idiot, as he saw it, he decided to go private. (Anon)

Almost any change in educational policy will see the numbers of children being educated privately go up or down, and the 1940s were no exception. Although trade was picking up briskly for the more expensive type of independent school, the private sector was a little jittery in the late 1940s, because of a proposal made by a report in 1944; the same year that the Butler Act was passed.

The Fleming Report, or, to give it its full and correct title, the Report of the Committee on Public Schools appointed by the President of the Board of Education, was the findings of an investigation into Britain's public schools, which were, confusingly, the very best private schools in the country. When the new Labour government came to power in 1945, they promptly set about nationalising all sorts of things, from coal mines to hospitals. Grammar schools were virtually nationalised and there were some who felt that the public schools should go the same way.

The Fleming Report did not recommend anything other than that 25 per cent of places at public schools should be made available to children passing Local Education Authority scholarships. The state would then pay their fees and they would then go to schools such as Harrow and Eton. The only problem with the idea was that nobody at all wanted this to happen.

I must be one of the few to have taken a scholarship and won a place at a public school in the late 1940s. Not that I actually went there, but I was definitely offered the place. It would have meant boarding, which my parents didn't want, and not only that, the council put a lot of pressure on them to turn it down. My parents asked me if I wanted to go to a boarding school and I didn't, so that would have been the end of it anyway. Frankly, I'm not even sure how I came to sit the exam in the first place. The council ended up offering me a place at a grammar in the area and I am sure that it was just as good as the private boarding school would have been. I never heard of anybody who actually took up one of these places. (Glynn Mitchell)

An odd film was in fact made, telling the fictionalised story of one such young man. It was called *The Guinea Pig* and starred Richard Attenborough as a working-class London boy who wins a place at an exclusive boarding school. He has a rough time of it, but ends up being offered a place at Cambridge; which news he greets with the words, 'Gosh, jolly good show!' This indicates the tremendous progress he has made in the years he has spent at the school.

In 1948, the public schools offered 580 places to children who passed scholarship examinations set by their local authority. Only 155 of these places were taken up. The whole scheme dragged on for a few years before grinding to a halt and being quietly abandoned.

What was wrong with the idea of opening up the public schools to ordinary children who won scholarships? The schools themselves were not very enthusiastic. The sort of parents who sent their children there did so, among other reasons, because the exclusivity was part of the attraction. Local authorities were not keen because they would have to pay the fees for the children. In contrast to the later assisted places scheme, where the government in Westminster picked up the bill, no arrangement had been made for state bursaries in the Fleming Report. Not unnaturally, local education authorities preferred to spend any money on their own schools.

My father talked of Atlee as though he were some sort of communist. Everything being nationalised and now the man had some crazy idea about sending crossing sweepers to Eton or some such nonsense! I was at Eton and remember him talking like this during the holidays. Apart from any educational benefit, my father knew that I was meeting the right sort of boy at Eton and would not be exposed to any yobbos. This is what he was paying for. It would have rather defeated the object of the exercise if anybody from a council estate could go there. (James R. Harker)

There was a very real fear at that time, in the late 1940s, that Labour might decide to nationalise the independent schools; treat them the way that they had the grammars. I didn't really know what all the fuss was about, but my parents were worried about it. The way they talked, you would have thought that a Bolshevik coup was in the offing. I had friends locally who didn't go to private schools and I couldn't see what would be so terrible if some of them came to my own school. (Anon)

For those struggling to pay school fees for a child at a grammar school before the war, the 1944 Education Act was something of a boon. If their child was reasonably bright, it meant that he could still go to the grammar school and the only difference was that the place would now be free. The wealthier, though, cut their ties with the grammar schools and plumped entirely for independent schools for their children.

> When I went to boarding school in 1947, it was absolutely heaving with new people. Speaking to some of them, one gathered that the decision to send them away to school had been made rather hurriedly. Certainly a few of them had expected to be going to grammar schools and then suddenly been packed off to boarding schools. I have an idea that this was caused by the opening up of the grammar schools to everybody. Some parents just didn't want to take any chances of their precious darlings being contaminated by coming into contact with ordinary children. It took a year or two for people to realise that it was really going to be business as usual at the grammars, with much the same sort of children going there. At first, I think some parents were worried that they would become like elementary schools. (Patrick J. McGuire)

There has never been a time when more than a small percentage of children in this country were being educated at independent schools. Despite their prominence in the national psyche during the post-war years, only a relatively tiny number of children were attending such schools.

The First Comprehensives

Comprehensive schools were first known as 'multilaterals' or 'common schools', up until the 1960s. However, not everyone was keen on the idea of a 'one size fits all' school in the years following the end of the Second World War.

> My father was a trade union shop steward, life-long Labour Party member; he was as left wing as they come. He had been a scholarship boy in East London and went to the Coopers School. He was as passionate as you could hope to be about grammar schools. He made damn sure that I passed my 11-plus and to him, this was how working people could get on in the world. (Glynn Mitchell)

> We lived in Hackney, just round the corner from Woodberry Down. I remember when it opened, my parents were horrified. They thought it was the beginning of the end; a school where everybody was mixed in together. There was no telling what awful habits I would pick up at such a place. I failed the 11-plus, so Woodberry Down, which was one of the first comprehensives, would have been where I was going. My father wouldn't hear of it and they managed to scrape together enough for me to go to a private girls' school in Camden. For them, a comprehensive was just like a glorified secondary modern. (Caroline T. Maxted)

Woodberry Down in Hackney was to be the future of secondary schooling in Britain. It opened in 1955 to much acclaim. It would reduce inequalities and unfairness by providing specialised, tailor-made education for each child. This at least was the theory. The first head of Woodberry Down, Mrs Chetwynd, claimed rashly that the educational opportunities at her school would be the equal of any grammar school. Many parents were unconvinced.

New comprehensives such as Holland Park in Notting Hill, and Tulse Hill, on the other side of London, tried to combine the best features of grammar schools and technical schools. On the one hand, they offered the opportunity to study Latin and Greek, on the other they were equipped with woodwork and metalwork rooms for those whose interests took a more practical line; the sort of children who might wish to begin an apprenticeship on leaving school, rather than going to university. One objection made about schools of this kind, even before any had been built, was that they would necessarily be very large; far larger than the secondary schools which already existed. Tulse Hill, for instance, had over 2,000 pupils. It could hardly be otherwise, if this one school was going to provide for the needs of all children in the catchment area.

> My parents lived near Holland Park and all their friends were sending their children to independent schools. There was a big fuss when it was announced that some old house was to be knocked down and a new school built on the site. This was right next to Holland Park itself; the horror! John Betjeman led the opposition to the building of the new school. My parents were socialists and although they were well able to afford a private education for me, they decided to send me to Holland Park when it opened. So, I went from a nice prep school to this huge new comprehensive. I loved it; I'm sure it was as good as any grammar school could have been. I lost a lot of my friends from the prep school, but made quite a few new ones who were from quite a different background to me. It was the best thing my parents could have done. (Anon)

To begin with, the new comprehensives had a rigorous streaming system, just like the most academic grammar school. Holland Park, for instance, graded children as A, B, C, D and E, but there were so many pupils that even these streams had to be subdivided further. After a few years of this, it was decided that it would be more egalitarian and less damaging to the self-esteem of pupils if this crude method of categorising them were abandoned, and the A, B and C streams were renamed H, P and S; for the initials of Holland Park School. It is not known how many of the pupils were taken in by this cunning piece of deception!

Strangely enough, the very first purpose-built comprehensive school to open in this country came about not as a result of some ideological commitment, but was built for purely practical reasons. In 1949, Britain's first comprehensive school began taking pupils. It had only been completed a few months earlier and was on the Welsh island of Anglesey and was called Holyhead County School. Local authorities had decided that it was not practical for them to operate a two-tier education system, with two lots of different secondary schools, and as a result built the comprehensive school.

> I grew up on Anglesey and didn't travel far from there as a child, only to towns in north Wales. The comprehensive was all that I knew, but when as a teenager I began to see more and more people who didn't live on Anglesey, they were amazed to hear that there was a place nearby that didn't have grammar schools and secondary moderns. They couldn't get over it. 'What, you mean everybody goes to the same school?' they used to ask. It worked very well at my school. The brainy ones took GCEs and others concentrated on metalwork and such like. I don't think any of us suffered from it. The funny thing is it wasn't at all planned. It just seemed to the council that it made more sense to have just the one big school. (Anon)

Although nobody realised it at the time, this was to be the future of education in this country. However, for most people back then, the grammar and secondary moderns were here to stay for the foreseeable future, and any other school was deemed strange.

> I remember when I was at the grammar school, my parents read in the papers of a new sort of secondary school, one which would teach all children together, regardless of how clever they were. They thought it sounded a terrible scheme. The only way that they could see it was in terms of grammar school pupils like their son being forced to mix in with all the secondary modern boys. The whole 11-plus business had only been going for ten years or so at that time, but for my mother and father it was now 'how things were' and as

such should be preserved at all costs. I think that in general, those who had kids at grammar school wanted to keep things the way they were, while a lot of people whose children had failed the 11-plus had a sense of grievance about the selective system and wanted to see it change. (Josephine A. Wilson)

If some people thought of the new comprehensives as being somewhat strange, there were other schools running at this time which could perhaps be described as 'crank schools'. Steiner schools, for instance, and those who ran unconventional or revolutionary schools at that time, were widely viewed as being crackpots and cranks; one such school was Summerhill Boarding School, started in 1921 by A.S. Neill.

At Summerhill, the children were free to attend lessons or not, entirely as the mood took them. Neill thought that he had discovered many wonderful things about the nature of childhood and learning, but few agreed with him. There were one or two other schools of this kind during the fifteen years or so after the end of the war, but none ever proved really popular.

Summerhill School was so much at odds with practically any other school running in Britain during the late 1940s that it really does deserve to be looked at in a little detail. Many of the ideas espoused by its controversial head would eventually come to be accepted as being perfectly sensible. Neill was fiercely opposed to corporal punishment, for example, and this has become the prevailing educational view in this country. He believed that it would be a good thing if schools were to be allowed to hand out contraceptives to adolescents, and this too is now common practice in many state schools. In a sense, the 'progressive' has now become the norm.

In other ways though, not least from an educational view, Summerhill was less satisfactory. The children might have been free from the rules and constraints imposed upon practically every other child in Britain at that time, but was this a good thing for them? Here is Neill, talking about the problem of bullying in his school:

In disciplined schools a boy is afraid to bully, but in a free school in which punishment by staff is out, to deal with a bully is not easy. Most bullies are rather stupid. The bright lad hits back with repartee, but the dunce can only use his fists. I have time and again felt that a boy who makes smaller boys afraid should not be in the school, but I did nothing about it, mainly because I could not think of a school to which he could go without being harshly treated.

An American named Max Bernstein tracked down some ex-pupils from Summerhill and found that the accusation that they had not been protected from bullies was raised by several of the former pupils. This seems to be borne out by the recollections of one man who was at the school just after the end of the war.

A couple of years after I left Summerhill, a boy who had been there at the same time got in touch with me and urged me to read a new children's book called *The Silver Chair* [a novel from C.S. Lewis's Narnia series]. He said it contained a very neat description of our old school. I think to this day that 'Experiment House' must certainly have been based on Summerhill! Not only were the bullies able to do what they wished without the staff intervening, but what Lewis says happened if one did come to the attention of the head. He said, 'All sorts of things, horrid things, went on which at an ordinary school would have been found out and stopped in half a term; but at this school they weren't. Or even if they were, the people who did them were not expelled or punished. The head said they were interesting psychological cases and sent for them and talked to them for hours. And if you knew the right sort of things to say to the head, the main result was that you became rather a favourite than otherwise.' This is Summerhill to a tee. Neill always seemed to have all the time in the world to talk to the bad boys, but didn't always see what went on out of his sight. (Anon)

With the emphasis always being upon the freedom of the child, it was perhaps inevitable that some children would feel that they were free to bully. The question of the freedom of the bullied children never seems to have been fully addressed.

The Ministry of Education, by and large, intensely disliked schools like Summerhill; progressive schools where children were not coerced into doing things that they did not wish to do. This lack of coercion even extended to lessons. The children at Summerhill had complete freedom of choice as to whether they actually learned anything while

An elementary class photograph in the North of England on Empire Day, 1938. (Courtesy Fred C. Palmer)

A class photograph of pupils from Roseworth Secondary Modern School in Stockton, 1959. (Courtesy Stockton Library Services)

Above: Pupils were expected to write with a pencil before progressing to a dip pen.

Opposite: Children sitting outside their primary school in 1949. (Courtesy Lindosland)

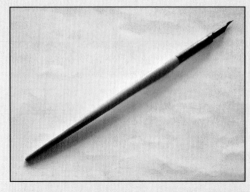

Left: A dip pen. Used with ink, it could often be a messy result!

Below left: A tawse, more commonly used as a tool to discipline unruly schoolchildren in Scotland. (Courtesy Picfreak)

Below: A school desk with a sloping lid and inkwell from the 1940s.

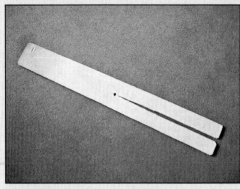

Opposite: Weavers Field School in Bethnal Green, London – a Victorian Board School in the Queen Anne mansion style.

A typical school satchel. (Courtesy Mark Hillary)

A grammar school cap.
(Courtesy Russ Hamer)

A grammar school girl in uniform, 1950. (Courtesy Snowstorm in Eastern Asia)

Portrack Primary School in Stockton, 1954.

A group of happy children, complete with caps and blazers, are waved off to boarding school.

they were at the school. Such an attitude would obviously have been anathema to a government school inspector! (Anon)

Little wonder that the inspectors were dismayed at a school where lessons were voluntary and some children were unable to read at twelve. This would be cause for concern even in today's more liberal and enlightened times; in the 1940s it was thought to be little short of neglect and abuse.

> I went to a tiny private school until I was eleven, which would have been in 1952. Private schools at that time had to be registered, but they didn't need to provide a minimum level of education. The school I was in didn't really give me any education at all. There was a lot of dancing and also mime. We skipped round in circles out of doors in the spring and then pretended to be daffodils or trees. I think that the head, a completely dotty woman, was a fan of Rudolf Steiner. She read us lots of fairy stories and told us about the spirit world. One thing that she and the two teachers never seemed to get round to was teaching any of us to read and write. I think they were afraid that it would stunt our creativity. My father had been to a similar sort of school himself and he became a painter. In the end, his parents paid for me to go to a proper school, where they were appalled at my ignorance and lack of education. Still, it doesn't seem to have done me any harm and I bet I enjoyed my early years a lot more than those children who had to sit indoors all day crouched over desks. (Anon)

Talking of 'crank' or progressive schools, we should really mention a state school which many at the time felt fell into this category. This was a secondary modern in the east end of London. It opened in 1945 and was run by a man called Alexander Bloom, whom some saw as the state school equivalent of A.S. Neill. St George's-in-the-East was in Stepney, then a notoriously rough part of the East End.

Alexander Bloom strongly disapproved of some of the routine features to be found in almost every school in the year that the war ended. Corporal punishment, competition, marks; Bloom found them all distasteful and was determined from the start that they should play no part in his school. The pupils at the school devised their own curriculum and were active in decisions about what should be taught in the school. Their head felt that having failed their 11-plus, many of the children who were enrolled at St George's-in-the-East already felt that they were failures, a belief which he hoped to remove.

The surprising thing was that such methods seem to work with children whom many others had already mentally consigned to the educational scrapheap. Alexander Bloom's methods did not catch on generally, but whenever wild generalisations were being made about secondary modern pupils, his brave experiment showed that not all secondary moderns were dumping grounds for the slow-witted and idle.

> I was at St George's in the late 1940s. The head, Alex Bloom, was absolutely amazing. He treated us as though we were at the best public school in Britain. We were trusted to behave sensibly and take charge of our own lives. Nobody ever got caned. I had friends at other secondary moderns in London and the teachers there were fighting like lion tamers to control the kids. It's hopeless to carry on like that, there are always more pupils than teachers and if you make it a competition to see who can be most awkward and cause the most trouble, then the kids are bound to win hands down every time. Mr Bloom didn't try to do that at all and neither by and large did the teachers. We worked together and everybody tried to make it work; which it did. (Harry R. Smith)

Attending school has, contrary to what most people believe, never been compulsory in this country. It is education which is compulsory and it was that which was specifically stated in the 1944 Education Act. Section 36 of the Act states that parents must cause their children to receive an efficient, full-time education, 'either by regular attendance at school or otherwise'. Of course, wealthy parents had for many years been in the habit of engaging governesses for their children and it was for this reason that the clause was added which explicitly allowed education to be otherwise than in school. The present Queen of England of course was educated in this way and did not attend school for a single day.

The new educational system which was brought in after the Second World War did not suit all parents and some decided to take the 1944 Education Act at its word and educate their children by other means than that of school. These were not well-to-do families who wished to hire governesses or tutors, but ordinary parents who wanted to take responsibility for their children's education. This home education was not popular with the authorities

In 1952, Mrs Joy Baker in Norfolk decided to take control of her children's education and stop sending them to school. This became something of a cause célèbre, with Norfolk Council going to the most extraordinary lengths to force Mrs Baker to return her children to school. At various times, she was prosecuted and her children taken into care. It took her the best part of a decade to prove the point, but eventually the courts were compelled to concede that she was perfectly correct and the law did allow for this type of education. A handful of other parents were doing the same thing as Mrs Baker during the 1940s and '50s. Some were taken to court and forced to send their children to school, others managed to evade notice. This was the beginning of the home education movement in Britain, which has seen the number of children being taught at home rise to tens of thousands today.

Discipline

We had one teacher when I was eleven and he was an absolute devil. If he was annoyed with somebody, perhaps because they were looking out of the window and not paying attention, he would throw the blackboard rubber at the child. For those who haven't seen such a thing, the blackboard rubber was a wooden thing, about the size and shape of a large scrubbing brush. Mostly, this would catch the kid a crack on the head or miss altogether, but on one occasion, it hit this boy right in the face and gave him a black eye. His mother came up to complain. Somehow the headmaster smoothed it over, but he must have spoken to Mr Thomas, because that was the last time he ever chucked the board rubber at us. (Ronald G. Feeney)

Then of course there were the serious punishments involving the cane.

In books, there is always something faintly amusing about somebody being given 'six of the best'. The reality was quite literally torture. It felt like somebody pressing a red hot poker against your backside. It may have been treated humorously in stories about Billy Bunter, but I never knew anybody threatened with six strokes of the cane to be anything other than terrified. I certainly don't remember anybody making any jokes about being thrashed like this; at least, not while they were actually at school. (Gregory Parker)

I was at a grammar school from 1949 to 1956. The cane was used quite a lot, especially with the first, second and third years; not so much with the older boys. Any of the teachers could cane you, which took place in the corridor or any convenient empty room. It was always just you and the master present, unless the offence had been jointly committed, in which case you might be there with one or two other boys. The usual number of strokes was two or three. I only ever received the famous 'six of the best' on one occasion. Six strokes of the cane is pure agony. The cane wasn't reserved for especially bad offences, you could get it for not doing homework or just mucking about in class. (Glynn Mitchell)

My parents were great ones for 'spare the rod and spoil the child'. The teachers at the schools I went to in the 1950s felt the same way – you could only get a child to do as they were told by hitting them. If I was caned at school, I would never tell my parents, because they would have given me another thrashing on top of it. I don't think that it made us better though. All it did was teach children to be cunning and deceitful. The things that went on at that school when the teachers weren't around, well you wouldn't believe it. The important thing was not so much to behave kindly and like decent people, but not to get caught. (Keith J. Ballard)

Viewing corporal punishment as the only way of teaching children how to behave and that it was being done ultimately for their own benefit was sometimes just a justification for hitting children because they were a nuisance.

I was caned a lot at school, by two masters in particular. I don't believe for a moment that I was a very disruptive boy at twelve, but some masters took a dislike to certain boys and I am convinced that they just looked for a chance to beat those they didn't care for. This was always the danger when any teacher could cane anybody they wanted. These beatings weren't being given because they wished to correct my evil ways; it was because they didn't like me and wanted to hurt me. Later on, around 1957, things changed and the new head became the only one who could cane boys. This was a much fairer system, because if you were sent to him by a teacher, he would ask for your side of what happened and didn't automatically get the cane out. It stopped the private vendettas that some masters had against certain boys. (James H. Schneider)

The amount of corporal punishment varied greatly from school to school. In some, the cane was held in reserve for the very worst of offences; in others it was wielded freely, even for minor infractions of school rules such as not handing in homework on time or talking in class. It was always used far more freely against boys than it was against girls. Children as young as eight and as old as eighteen were beaten for disobedience.

When I was eight, our class had been left unattended for a few minutes while the teacher, Miss Thirsk, was called away. She had left her handbag on the desk and a couple of boys, very daringly, went up to the front of the class to peer into it. I was showing off and went up there as well. They must have heard the teacher coming back, because by the time I was bending down and squinting into the handbag, they were back in their seats and Miss Thirsk walked back into the room. I have never seen anybody so angry. She told me to go to the office and fetch the cane and the book. All punishments with the cane had to be recorded. I was trembling with fear when I returned, and she told me to put my hand out and gave me one very hard slash across my palm. It was horribly painful. (Paul M. Richardson)

I was at a Jesuit school. I stayed until the sixth, leaving in 1954 to go to university. Although the school was near London, they had a very traditional Scottish form of punishment; the tawse. This was a long leather strap, dived into two tongues. It was used pretty freely by the teachers. When I was in the upper sixth (I was eighteen) our class was in a restless mood one day, not concentrating and with low level disruptions. The teacher was fed up with it and announced sternly, 'If I hear another peep out on anybody, I shall fetch the tawse.' Inevitably, I said 'Peep' quietly. It was not so quiet that he didn't hear and true to his word, he went and got the tawse. At the age of eighteen, I then had to bend over his desk for two strokes with the tawse. Eighteen! (Keith J. Ballard)

The tawse was used in Scotland in preference to the cane. Some schools in the north of England also adopted the tawse, but it was unusual to hear of its being used as far south as London.

Only punishments with the cane were officially recorded in 'the book'. It was not at all uncommon for teachers to use rulers and plimsolls to inflict instant chastisement in the classroom. Many of these punishments were for astonishingly trivial things such as leaving one's seat without permission.

> I remember being struck on the hand with the ruler for talking in class. I had just been asking the boy next to me if I could borrow a rubber. (Harry R. Smith)

> When I was in the last year of juniors, there was a queue for the drinking fountain in the playground. A boy nipped in front of me when it was my turn and I called him a 'Bloody cheat'. He told on me and the teacher on duty told me to see him at going home time. He told me that he had never heard of such disgusting language in all his life and that I deserved to be punished. I had to bend over the table and he gave me three blows with a slipper. (Glynn Mitchell)

To be fair to the teachers, class sizes in the 1940s and '50s were absolutely enormous compared with today. Forty-five was common in primary schools and fifty not exceptional. Each teacher was solely in charge, with no help from teaching assistants. Keeping control of such large numbers of children was not easy and the threat of physical punishment probably helped to keep pupils in order.

At some secondary moderns, anything short of a beating with the cane was regarded by some of the pupils – particularly boys – as being a sign of weakness on the part of the masters. Here is a joke, which, nevertheless has an element of truth in it. A new headmaster was appointed to a particularly wild boys' secondary modern. At the first assembly, he announced that he was trying a new form of discipline in the school. 'From now on,' he said, 'any boy caught breaking the rules will be sent to me for a warning. If he is caught again, he will receive a second warning. Only after a third offence will he be properly punished.' The boys could hardly disguise their delight at this news and one boy said to his friend, in a voice loud enough to be heard on the stage, 'We've got a right soft one here, Harry.' The headmaster ordered him up onto the stage, bent him over the table and thrashed him thoroughly with the cane. He then declared, 'Right. That was your first warning!'

Of course, not all punishment was physical. In grammar schools, the giving of lines was common, as was the delivering of an 'imposition' – the writing of an essay or copying out of passages in Latin, for instance. Even in secondary moderns though, the threat of the cane was still ever-present.

> The prefects at our grammar school had the right to give out impositions, known colloquially as 'impots'. These could be lengthy projects which would mean having to research some obscure subject in the school library. Instead of playing with your friends at lunchtime, you would be looking things up in the library. This was pretty effective; at least it kept you out of mischief for a while. (David P. Taylor)

> I have thought in recent years that the way we were treated at school had a lot of similarities with what you read about the brainwashing of prisoners of war in Korea. I am talking now about the same period as the Korean War, the early 1950s. Our individual identities were removed by making us all dress the same, there was unremitting discipline and being marched about in groups and not encouraged to think for ourselves. Then there were the random and savage punishments, designed to strike fear into us and make us nervous. By the third year at grammar school, we were all pretty well broken in a sense. (Glynn Mitchell)

This attitude, that each person should surrender autonomy and became little more than a cell in a larger organism, was explicitly stated by many schools to be a desirable state of affairs. It was also idealised in many children's books during the 1940s and '50s. It is revealing to glance at the work of that most enduringly popular of children's writers, Enid Blyton. Blyton's stories, especially those dealing with life at school, are full of children and young people who begin with quirky and distinctive characters but after undergoing various unpleasant and often humiliating experiences come to realise that true happiness is to be found in conforming to the *mores* of the group. In Blyton's books, such surrendering of individual personality is often accompanied by mention of corporal punishment.

In *The Naughtiest Girl in the School*, Elizabeth Allen learns to do as everybody else does. She is at a boarding school where the rule is that each child may only have six items on top of her chest of drawers. Elizabeth places eleven objects on top and is then punished when a monitor confiscates five of the items, including a treasured photograph of Elizabeth's parents. This sort of casual cruelty is portrayed as being very right and proper and the correct way to teach a child to conform to the rules. Later on in *The Naughtiest Girl in the School*, the same monitor threatens, 'Get dressed and hurry up or I'll spank you with a hairbrush! Monitors do that sometimes you know.'

Obedience to rules and physical punishment is shown to be good for children in Enid Blyton's stories and held up as an example to be followed. Both in their day-to-day life and in the books which they read, children were constantly reminded that being a good pupil at school consisted of doing precisely as one was told and not expressing any desire to do or say anything at all out of the ordinary.

There were so many rules at my secondary school that it was quite impossible to remember them all. Lower forms had to come in by one door, sixth formers by another and there was a separate entrance for masters. We had to walk on the left-hand side of the corridor; no running indoors; no raising one's voice; and uniform had to be precisely right, even down to the colour of our socks. Any breaking of rules could mean being given a conduct mark. If you accumulated three conduct marks in a week that earned you a detention. Five detentions in a term meant a caning, as did any subsequent detention once the fifth had been given. This system gave endless scope for bullying by prefects and masters of those whom they disliked. Absolutely everybody forgot to walk on the prescribed side of the corridor or sometimes broke into a run if they were late. If it was a boy who was not disliked, the master might say something like, 'Slow down, Williams.' If, on the other hand, it was a notorious troublemaker, he would be given a conduct mark. The consequence was that the same boys ended up with loads of detentions every term and the canings which resulted. It was a grossly unfair system. (Conrad Summerfield)

A term didn't pass without my being caned for one reason or another. I don't think that I was a particularly rebellious boy, but I would not follow what seemed to me mad regulations. One beating I got at the grammar school I attended sticks in my memory. Our school had two quadrangles with roses in them. These were enclosed on all sides by the classrooms. If you were in a hurry, it was far quicker to nip across these quads from one corridor to the other. Except, of course, this was a privilege reserved for masters and prefects. I was nearly late for a class once and we were of course forbidden to run in the corridors. I decided to risk cutting through the quad and ran straight into the head. He recognised me at once and told me to see him at break. I was caned. This small incident sums up for me all that was wrong with schools of that sort in the 1950s: the slavish obedience to tradition, the cruelty and the snobbishness. (Paul M. Richardson)

I was once caned for literally nothing! The master who caned me was an ex-army man and while he was giving me a dressing down over some shortcoming, I said nothing at all, but just stared at him; looked him in the eye. This was enough for him – he caned me for what he called 'dumb insolence'. Dumb insolence! In other words, doing and saying nothing at all, but merely looking as though one might be thinking insolent thoughts. This is not *Alice in Wonderland*, it is more *Nineteen Eighty Four*; thought crime. (John B. Fleming)

School discipline was not restricted to the school premises, but extended into the world outside the school. As long as you were wearing uniform, you could be called to account for your behaviour to and from school. A pupil seen smoking in the street by a teacher could be punished at school, and many schools were very strict about how children should behave in public, even when the school day had officially ended.

I remember getting into terrible trouble because I pushed to the front of the queue for a bus. There were murmurs of annoyance from the people waiting in the queue, but I didn't realise that one of them was our caretaker. He reported me to the head and I was given a hefty imposition. This meant a long essay that I had to research and write in my own time. That kept me busy during lunchtime for the week. I was silly enough to tell my parents about how unfair I thought it was and they backed the head all the way. They were disgusted at the idea of queue jumping. This was only a couple of years after the end of the war and queue jumping in those days was practically a hanging matter. (James H. Schneider)

This neatly illustrates another big difference between the way things were for schoolchildren in the post-war years and how they are now. Parents supported the teachers almost unconditionally, taking their word for it if it was claimed that their child had deserved punishment. Children knew this and so, faced with a unified front of adult authority, seldom tried to play off their parents against their teachers.

It was in the early summer of 1957. I was fourteen and had been smoking regularly for perhaps a year. Me and my friends bought ten Players at the tobacconist near the school and then lit up as we walked home. The maths teacher saw us and the next day at school we were summoned to his room. He gave us a choice of being caned or being suspended for a couple of days and having our parents called in to the school. It was no contest really and we took the caning. Even then, I thought it a little bit like sharp practice, to punish us for something perfectly legal which everybody in the country did anyway, just because we were on the way home from school. (John B. Fleming)

The rationale behind it was that when a boy or girl was in uniform, they represented the school and that bad behaviour reflected not just on the individual concerned, but also on the school itself.

I went to a convent school and we were not even supposed to talk to boys on the way home. This rule included, bizarrely enough, even our own brothers! The reason for this, as the nuns explained, was that people in the street would not know that the boy was our brother and it might still give the impression that we were a little lax morally to be seen chatting shamelessly in public with a young man. A crisis occurred when we were rehearsing a play near Christmas. We were putting it on at the Campion's School, which was a strict Jesuit school for boys. The dangerous experiment was allowing Ursuline girls and Campion's boys to act on stage together. Just before the play was performed, a girl was seen walking near the school, chatting as bold as brass with a young man. She explained to the Reverend Mother that he was a Campion's boy and that they had been planning something to do with the play. She got away with it, although everybody in her class new that he was really her boyfriend from the local technical college. (Josephine A. Wilson)

When I was first at school, I used to get into trouble a lot, until I worked out that the main thing was not getting caught out by teachers and prefects. I became something of an expert at sailing close to the wind and not getting caught. When I was at secondary school, which was 1948 to 1953, there were a million little rules and getting caught breaking any of them could result in a thrashing. I found that I enjoyed the risk of breaking the rules, with the danger of being beaten if I was found out. It's only in recent years that I have thought that my business life was very much like that; the thrill of getting away with things that would result in heavy penalties if I were caught. I think it all dates back to how I learned to be at school. (Glynn Mitchell)

I was at a convent school, a boarding school in the early 1950s. I cannot tell you how many stupid little rules there were, not only about how we had to behave, but even what we were to think and feel. Having control exercised to this degree over adolescent girls cannot be a healthy thing and many of the girls with whom I was at school reacted as soon as they had left by launching into what I can only call hazardous and unconventional lifestyles. (Anon)

From my earliest days at school, I have had an absolute horror of being exposed to criticism by reason of my conduct. At our school – I am talking here about the later 1940s, early 1950, they had a very effective method of dealing with troublesome girls. You were made to stand on a chair in the dining room while everybody was eating. It doesn't sound a very severe punishment compared with some schools where children were being caned, but it was sheer agony. This only happened to me once, but it made a very deep impression upon me and I made very sure that I never did anything which would draw unfavourable attention to me again while I was at school. This became a habit which has stayed with me ever since. (Dorothy Dobson)

I have always been one for keeping rules, no matter how petty or unimportant. I have never been able to disregard a notice or walk on grass where a sign tells me to keep off. This is not a conscious thing; it is rather part of my very being. My parents were real sticklers for doing as you were told and my school, I suppose, reinforced this. I was a very well behaved child from the moment I started school, not at all the sort to get into trouble. I think that I thrived on all those rules. At least I knew just what I needed to do to get approval. I am talking now of the first years after the war. We had to walk on one side of the corridor, not run, speak quietly, wear our uniforms just so. I have been exactly the same all my life, trying to find out what the rules are and then following them. On the whole, it's worked very well for me. (Peter A. Barker)

School discipline fifty or sixty years ago was very strict and many people carried the effects of this early training with them for the rest of their lives. The very experience of living for years under the threat of physical violence, which was essentially the case in schools at that time, cannot fail to have a powerful effect on young children's minds. From starting school at five, until leaving at anything from fifteen to eighteen, children and young people were liable to be slapped, pushed, grabbed and struck with various implements; ranging from slippers to canes and tawses.

It could be argued that corporal punishment was necessary to maintain order in schools where one young teacher could easily be in sole control of fifty children for hours at a time; nevertheless, it was hardly an ideal state of affairs. Part of the difficulty was that government spending on state schools had not been high until the passing of the 1944 Education Act. A natural consequence was that school buildings became dilapidated over the years and there was insufficient numbers of staff. This meant large classes and not enough teachers to cope with them. Disciplining those who caused trouble was probably the easiest way of keeping order.

Relaxation of discipline generally did not begin to take place until the 1960s were well under way. As the 1950s drew to a close though, things were changing. Educational theories were changing towards 'child-centred' education, and British schools were becoming more humane places altogether.

It is over twenty years since the cane and every other form of corporal punishment in state schools was abolished. There is no evidence at all that this state of things was better for children than the methods of discipline now employed and, sadly, there is good reason to think that many children were harmed psychologically by the practice.

Apart from the beatings which were dished out quite freely at schools in the 1940s and '50s, other degrading punishments were not that uncommon.

I remember the routine for any boy who forget his games kit on the mornings that we had PE. The master in charge was an ex-army instructor and he used to regard the forgetting of one's kit as a direct challenge to his authority. The culprit was compelled to strip down to his vest and pants and run round the playing field. I have seen boys made to do this even in the winter. To be fair, it taught you to make sure that you didn't forget your kit and few boys needed more than one such session. Imagine such a thing happening today; you would have people going to the court of human rights about it! (Paul M. Richardson)

At my convent school, which was a grammar, the punishments varied between the sensible and the raving mad and sadistic. An example of the former was getting girls to collect litter and tidy up the playground. This kept them out of mischief and made them useful. The strangest punishment which I ever witnessed was a very bold and rebellious girl who was set to scrubbing some steps with an old toothbrush. This was a soul-destroying and pointless task. I heard later that it was one of the things that the novice nuns were subjected to and so perhaps this is why they thought it was a good idea. (Josephine A. Wilson)

Counting the daisies on the playing field! I was sent out to do this on several occasions. It seems utterly mad today and yet it was the kind of thing which was I suppose intended to break our spirits. It was not enough to wander round like Wordsworth, admiring the flowers. You had to get down on your hands and knees for half an hour and actually look as though you were doing the job properly. (Glynn Mitchell)

Uniforms

I started in the infants in 1946 and left the secondary modern ten years later, in 1956. I didn't wear a uniform at all for any of that time. The only kids locally who wore a uniform were those from the grammar school. In infants, juniors and the secondary modern, none of us had a uniform. (Brenda Jacobs)

Today, there are hardly any schools which do not impose a uniform of some sort; even primary schools expect children to wear the same clothes to school, typically starting from the age of five. Because of this, we assume that most children wore uniforms sixty or seventy years ago. In fact, the situation with school uniforms was very different in the late 1940s from today. At the end of the Second World War, and for years afterwards, hardly any children wore a school uniform.

There were no uniform requirements for the old elementary schools, for the simple reason that most children at that time were living in conditions that we would today regard as poverty. Most children had one winter coat, one good pair of shoes, one pair of trousers and so on. It was these everyday clothes that they wore to school. This continued in primary schools long after the abolition of elementary schools. Well into the 1960s, children at junior schools were wearing their ordinary clothes to school. The only attempt at any sort of uniform might perhaps be to require boys to wear a tie in the school colours. What strikes us at once about such school photographs is that none of the children are wearing uniforms.

I left school in 1958. I did not wear a uniform at all at any stage. In juniors we were supposed to wear a school tie, but hardly anybody bothered. At the secondary modern, there was no uniform requirement at all, except a few things like not wearing jeans. Apart from that, we could wear what we pleased. I don't think my parents would have been able to afford blazers, caps and so on anyway. (Ronald G. Feeney)

There was no uniform for primary school. When I passed the 11-plus though, I knew that I would have to be kitted out with a proper uniform. It was expensive, but my parents were so proud that I was going to be going to the grammar school that they didn't mind scrimping and saving a bit to make sure I looked the part. Shorts, blazer, smart shoes, shirt, tie, gabardine raincoat, cap; the whole works. It was this which set us apart from the kids at the secondary modern. They wore what they wanted, but we were always smartly turned out. You could tell at once if somebody had passed the 11-plus by what they wore to school. (Keith J. Ballard)

The parents of children who passed their 11-plus were often very proud of the fact that their child would be wearing a school uniform. For the first few years after the 1944 Education Act came into force, nothing much changed as far as school uniforms were concerned. Towards the end of the 1950s, though, some secondary moderns were trying to copy the grammar schools by introducing uniforms. The universal custom of primary school children being dressed in uniforms did not come until much later. In a way, it made sense for those at secondary moderns to wear the clothes that they ordinarily wore. A few years earlier and many of these young people would have been going off to work. They did not really see themselves as schoolchildren and neither did their teachers in many cases. The case was quite different with the boys and girls at grammar schools and independent schools.

In addition to enforcing conformity, the school uniform was intended to remind pupils that they were under the supervision and control of teachers.

I stayed on in the sixth, leaving in the summer of 1949. Our grammar school was very conventional and we all wore old-fashioned gymslips. I have pictures of myself at that time and I look like an extra from a

St Trinian's film! Every detail of our clothing was precisely laid down by the rules, even down to our underwear. I think that part of the aim was to keep us looking and feeling like children and so make us easier to control. Certainly, we tended to be a lot more childish than eighteen-year-old girls who had left school and been at work for a few years. Wearing a uniform of this sort was all part of that. (Ellen T. Cade)

At our school, the rule was that until the third year all boys had to wear short trousers. This meant that at the age of thirteen, I was still travelling to and from school looking like a small boy. Those of my friends who had gone to the secondary modern were spared this indignity. I am sure that part of these ridiculous rules were concerned with trying to prevent any rebellion against the established order. Keeping teenagers dressed like this was a means to that end. (Keith J. Ballard)

Uniform was used in this way to reinforce and emphasise the school hierarchy. Pupils progressed through various stages and one could often tell at a glance just where in the scheme of things a pupil was, just by his or her appearance. In some girls' schools, for instance, the first year and possibly the second year pupils might be required to wear socks. After a certain age, other variations of the uniform might be permitted. In the sixth form, different blazers might be the uniform or caps might no longer be worn. The idea was to make the child fit in and look exactly the same as all the others in the year.

Independent schools usually made their pupils wear uniform from a much younger age. At prep schools, boys of seven or eight would be wearing a miniature version of the uniform which the older pupils wore. In 1950, a seven-year-old in school uniform and wearing a cap would almost certainly be from an independent school.

During the transitional period of the late 1940s, when the elementary schools were changing into secondary moderns, it was uncommon to find children at state schools wearing a uniform. As the 1950s passed, though, and the division between the grammar schools and the rest of the educational system became more noticeable, a number of secondary moderns introduced uniforms. Old photographs of the time reveal subtle differences in the uniforms adopted by the two kinds of educational establishment.

The grammar schools tried deliberately to copy the uniform requirements of the more expensive private schools; straw boaters for girls, caps
for boys, generally a smarter appearance overall. Even when uniforms
were introduced to secondary moderns, they tended to be more relaxed
and the pupils themselves were apt to wear them in unconventional ways.

> We had skirts that were supposed to be of a particular length; no more
> than an inch above the knee was the official ruling. These skirts were
> bought from the same outfitter as the girls' grammar, but we always
> managed to make them a little less respectable. At the grammar
> school, they really did look uniform, all having their skirts at the
> regulation length and looking very prim and proper. I think their
> teachers were pretty hot about skirt length. At our school, which
> was a secondary modern, we used to roll the skirts over at the top so
> that they were much shorter. Once in a while, a teacher would say
> something, but mostly they weren't bothered. It was the same with
> the boys. In the grammar school they were always neatly turned out,
> but somehow the boys at our school always managed to look scruffy.
> It was nothing you could put your finger on, but you could always tell
> who went to a secondary modern and who was at a grammar school.
> (Catherine E. Kinglsey)

It was some years later before primary schools began wearing uniforms.
Some of the Church schools required their pupils to wear uniform in the
juniors, but even with them it was not universal. At the state schools,
hardly any children under the age of eleven wore uniform, right up to the
1970s.

> At our school, the only rules to do with clothes was that boys were
> supposed to wear a tie in the school colours of black and gold. Some
> did and some didn't and none of the teachers used to bother about it.
> It wasn't really necessary to tell the girls how to dress, because there
> was already a set of conventions which we all followed. No trousers of
> course in the early 1950s, plain skirts in the winter and cotton frocks
> in the summer. If you look at my school photograph from those days,
> you would think that we were wearing a uniform; all the girls wearing
> cotton frocks, with cardigans and white ankle socks. I have to say we
> looked smart enough. (Lillian O. Drake)

There was a lot of debate during the 1950s regarding the advantages of having school uniforms. Some of the arguments which were in favour of the idea are still around today, for instance that it prevents poorer children being stigmatised because they are unable to keep up with the latest fashions. Many teachers felt that uniforms were good for discipline, and even today there are schools which make sure that the pupils have their ties knotted tight enough or their blazers on at all times.

The public schools of the nineteenth century ensured that their boys dressed in very distinctive styles. This was more to emphasise their superiority and social status than for any other reason. Grammar schools wishing to appear grand, adopted uniforms so that they could appear to be on the same footing as the public schools. From the grammars, the trend for uniform spread to secondary moderns, who wished to show that they were of equal status to grammars. For most of the 1940s and '50s though, the smarter the secondary school pupil in terms of uniform, the more likely it was that they attended grammar school. Pupils in working-class areas who had passed the 11-plus were very noticeable when they went to and from school, because their smart blazer and cap marked them out at once from all the other children of similar age.

> I used to take my cap off and stuff it in my pocket as soon as I was out of sight of the school. Where I lived, hardly any of the boys went to a grammar school and you could tell them at once because they were wearing caps. My mates in the street where I lived wouldn't care, but if I bumped into some boys from the secondary modern who didn't know me, they might try and knock off my cap or snatch it and run away with it. I used to wear my raincoat buttoned up well into the spring as well. This concealed my blazer, which in typical grammar school style was very distinctive with alternating dark and pale stripes. With just a gabardine on and no cap, I didn't look like a grammar school boy, which was a lot safer. (Glynn Mitchell)

> I went to the girls' county high school, and, like so many grammar schools, they seemed to go out of the way to make the uniform conspicuous. Ours was a bright green with yellow blouses. It looked utterly hideous and of course we could be seen coming down the

road for miles. The primary school pupils used to jeer at us and chant, 'Greengage and custard' when we passed them in the street. It was popularly thought that all grammar school girls were real snobs, but this was crazy. I had passed the 11-plus to get there and my own parents were as working class as they come. Still, that's how others saw us. (Ellen T. Cade)

By 1959, quite a few secondary moderns had also adopted uniforms and the secondary school without one was becoming something of an oddity. Most primary schools still didn't expect pupils to wear uniform, although some introduced uniforms which were optional. Today, schools without uniforms in this country are decidedly rare. In some counties, only one or two exist.

New Buildings and Old

Most of the elementary schools in Britain were old Victorian Board Schools. These were often built in a style known as Queen Anne Revival. It looks like an early eighteenth-century mansion, with gables, tall windows and details picked out in terracotta. Although it started to be used for elementary schools in London, this style spread rapidly to other British cities. Inside, a vast, echoing assembly hall was surrounded on three sides by classrooms. Typically, there were separate playgrounds and entrances for boys and girls. With three floors, such a building would accommodate all children from the age of five through to the age of fourteen, when they would leave. The infants would begin on the ground floor and then progress upwards as they grew older.

With a little ingenuity, the old Queen Anne Revival type of elementary school was adapted to accommodate the overhaul of the educational system in 1944. In other words, for many children there was no real change at all in where they were taught.

> I started at the infants at Downshall, which was a huge old barn of a place, dating back to the nineteenth century. The hall was also the gym and the place where we had plays and carol concerts. The classrooms were along the side of the hall. When I was seven, I went into the juniors, which was a newer building across the road. I failed my 11-plus, which meant that I went to Downshall secondary modern, which was based in the upper stories of the infants' school. My whole school career took place in the same place. (Harry R. Smith)

Today, it is more common for primary and secondary education to be separate. Up until the late 1950s though, there was no sharp division between primary and secondary. The child who went to Downshall infants then went on to Downshall juniors and progressed to Downshall secondary modern. All this would have taken place on the same site within the same Victorian building used for generations of pupils. Later, as the changes of the Butler Act gained pace, new buildings were erected.

Raising the school leaving age meant that in the new secondary modern schools, extra classrooms would be needed for the additional group of pupils aged from fourteen to fifteen. This would not be necessary in the grammar schools, which were already geared to the needs of pupils up to the age of eighteen. For the secondary moderns though, it was a significant problem. Using the former elementary schools for secondary education would be neither possible nor desirable in the long run. Here is what a former pupil has to say about Barnoldswick Secondary Modern.

> Even by the standards of the times, our school was pretty grim. It had been thrown up in a bit of a hurry and it showed. Some of the older schools were quite nice to look at, but this looked like something from an industrial estate. If it wasn't for the sign outside saying 'Barnoldswick Secondary Modern', you might have taken it for a factory – either that or a prison. (Brenda Jacobs)

The raising of the school leaving age had coincided with the so-called baby boom of the post-war years. Not only were thousands of fifteen-year-olds having to be accommodated in increasingly dilapidated buildings, there was a greater number of five-year-olds starting school, which resulted in larger class sizes.

> The local paper was kicking up a stink last year because my grand-daughter's school had classes of thirty-one pupils. Apparently this exceeds some government guideline or other. I couldn't help remembering my own days at that same school in the 1950s. I still have one of my old reports. It is from the summer of 1956 and there, in black and white, is the number of pupils in the class; fifty-two. There was only one young woman to keep control of us and teach us. There were no such things as classroom helpers in those days. I can see now

how difficult it was for those in charge of the school, because it had not been built to cater for so many children. The old part of the school is only used for offices now, and in the 1970s they built a huge new place nearby. With class sizes like that we weren't receiving a brilliant, personally tailored education and it's no wonder that hardly any of us passed the 11-plus. (Josephine A. Wilson)

To give some idea of what the buildings were like in one of the all-age sites of those times, here is a description of Dane School in Ilford, on the outskirts of London. In 1964, Ilford MP Tom Iremonger said:

The building is an old solid school board building built before 1904. It shares with a primary school an island site, the total area of which is less than 2 acres. On this island site there are 296 secondary modern girls, 314 secondary modern boys, 330 juniors and 223 infants, a total of 1,163 children.

Writing of this same school in 1957, HM Inspectors despaired:

This school offers notable examples of the triumphing of spirit over matter, of vision over material difficulties. The building and site seriously cramp the school, and it is doubtful whether they can ever be made adequate to serve the purposes of secondary education.

These two quotations make it perfectly clear that as late as the 1960s, the old, all-age elementary school was still flourishing in all but name.

I attended the infants and juniors at an absolutely massive old Victorian school. There were well over a thousand kids on the site, ranging in age from five to fifteen. If you failed the 11-plus, as most of the kids there did, you gradually progressed upwards. The infants and juniors were on the ground floor and the secondary modern on the upper floors. It had been an elementary school and was frankly a bit of a crumbling ruin. It was horribly overcrowded and the fabric of the building was in a shocking state; peeling paint, leaky windows that let in the rain, and no proper heating. I passed my 11-plus and was astonished at the difference when I got to the grammar school. It was clean and had a lovely library, even the textbooks were in better condition. I learned when I was older that the council didn't like spending money on the old secondary modern. (Glynn Mitchell)

Most of the state school buildings at the time had been built before the end of the nineteenth century, and some looked more like prisons or workhouses than modern schools. HM Inspectors regularly denounced the facilities in these schools, but little was done about them, at least not for many years.

> Our secondary modern was in a Victorian building. The only source of heating was coal fires in the classrooms. It was a huge old barn of a place. The ceilings were very high, which meant that any warmth from the fire just travelled up and became lost to us. Those classrooms were freezing in winter. The windows were the original ones as well. They were wooden and let in draughts even when they were closed. The conditions really didn't encourage you to sit and concentrate on your work. Our teacher used to turn a blind eye if some of us stood by the fire instead of getting on with our work. That was one good thing about the secondary modern; nobody took the school work there too seriously. (Catherine E. Kingsley)

There is no doubt that conditions in many of the old schools at this time were wretched. The overcrowding was eased to some extent by the newly built HORSA huts, but the conditions in the huts were not much better than those in the school itself. They were likely to let in wind and rain, and this was certainly the case with some of the new huts.

> The famous HORSA huts! We had half a dozen at our school and they were supposed to reduce overcrowding. Of course they did nothing of the sort, because they were all built in the same years that the school leaving age was raised. There were far more pupils after that and so the new buildings didn't reduce crowding at all. We had to cross the playground to get to them. Sometimes it was pouring with rain or even snowing. Some teachers would let us go to the cloakroom and get our coats, but others thought it was just an excuse for wasting time. So we would arrive in the hut cold, wet and irritable before the lesson had even begun. (Ronald G. Feeney)

In complete opposition to the run-down council-paid secondary modern school buildings, grammar schools were as comfortable and desirable as possible. Because they were privately run, more money was available for painting, decorating and so on.

> I know that some of the teachers at my school were bitter about how little money was available for doing the place up. They definitely felt that the nearby grammar school was favoured. I heard it said that this was because most of the councillors' children were at the grammar, but I don't know whether or not that is true. (Harry R. Smith)

As the 1950s progressed, it became obvious that the old Victorian buildings, which had served communities for generations, would not really do for the future and so began the construction of new secondary modern schools; schools fit for the twentieth century. Few of these were to be attractive structures. Many of the new schools were bleak and uncompromisingly functional in both design and appearance.

> I was one of the first year's intakes at the new secondary modern when it was built. It was hideous – yellow brick and with small windows. It looked like an enlarged version of the public toilets in the town centre. It was made of the same materials and probably built by the same crew, so that wasn't really surprising. It had better facilities than the old building, but was utterly soulless. Everything about it was simply practical. In the Victorian building we had been in before, there were little touches of individuality. Nothing much, just fancy ironwork here and there and terracotta scrolls around the doorways. There was nothing like that in the new school. (Brenda Jacobs)

> Our council was being encouraged to build a new school for the secondary modern pupils, but they felt that the old one had many years of useful life left in it yet. Their solution was to erect a concrete and glass block as an extension for the old school. It looked ghastly. There was this Queen Anne Revival-style school from 1880 or so, and stuck on one side was a modern office block. Still, it did give extra room and I'm sure that it was cheaper than knocking the old place down and starting from scratch. (John B. Fleming)

In the 1800s, when these buildings were erected, living standards were much lower than they were in the 1950s, and it was quite acceptable for children to spend their days in a cold building, heated only by one inadequate coal fire in each classroom. After all, the children in these elementary schools were quite used to being cold and sitting in draughts at home – there was no point making the industrial schools too luxurious. This may have been satisfactory in the closing years of Queen Victoria's reign, but it was not what many people were starting to expect after the end of the Second World War.

> The fires in the classroom just about took the chill from the air on a cold winter's day, but the hall had no heating at all. We were expected to strip to our knickers and vests for PE in the hall. No wonder so many of us ended up with chilblains. (Lillian O. Drake)

The first secondary moderns to be purpose-built were often designed to be functional rather than attractive, but this was not always the case. From the late 1950s onwards, some notable secondary schools were erected which were designed to be as modern and eye-catching as possible; breaking away entirely from the traditional ideas of schools as being draughty old barns with high ceilings. Some of these new schools were striking as examples of modern architecture in their own right. One such was Tulse Hill boys' comprehensive school, in the south London borough of Lambeth.

A massive, eight-storey glass-clad building with four lifts, Tulse Hill was to be the future of education in this country. It opened in 1956 and accommodated over 2,000 pupils – far more than any grammar or secondary modern. Tulse Hill was stupendously well equipped. Among other facilities, it boasted no fewer than six gymnasia and, of all unlikely things, a cinema organ in the main hall. This had been acquired from the old Gaumont cinema on Rose Hill and was used for the playing of hymns during assembly. Urban myth says that the cracks which had appeared in the walls of the old hall had been caused by the resonating low notes produced by the organ. Another legend had it that these cracks were there because the original architect's plans had been for a four-storey building, and that to save money, those in charge of construction had simply erected two such buildings, one on top of the other, thus creating the eight-storey building. Other new comprehensives were also being built towards the end of the 1950s, among them Holland Park and Woodberry Down in London.

> I remember a lot of school building going on during the 1950s. Bits were being tacked on to some of the old Victorian schools and completely new buildings were going up. When I went to the local secondary modern in 1946, it hadn't changed since it was built. Open fires, big draughty rooms with ill-fitting windows. By the time my brother went there in 1958, it was quite different. There were radiators instead of fires, special woodwork rooms and a brand new annex for arts and crafts. (Janet L. Thompson)

> I was one of the first pupils at the new secondary modern school built to replace the old Victorian building. It was a very exciting place, not like a school at all, more like a modern office block. There were music rooms, everything a proper school should have. It made a difference to how we thought about school. It gave the impression that the authorities thought that it was worth spending money on us. (Dorothy Dobson)

By 1960, it was obvious to many in the field of education that the future lay in comprehensive schools and the differing accommodation described above was becoming less noticeable. There is almost no difference at all these days in the facilities offered by grammar schools and comprehensives; a trend which was well under way by the end of the 1950s.

Catholic Schools

Since the seventeenth century, Britain has had a strong tradition of Catholic schools. These have often been associated with orders of nuns such as the Ursulines. Religious instruction in Catholic schools seeped into every nook and cranny of life; it was a constant presence in the lives of pupils.

We had various statues scattered about the school; Our Lady, St Francis and so on. We were supposed to treat these things with as much reverence as though they were real saints. You would automatically lower you voice when passing Our Lady, for example. When I started in the infants, I can still remember one of the first sentences we learned to write. It was 'God made the red apple.' Everything, literally everything, came back to the faith. Disobeying a nun was almost like rebelling against the Lord himself. Wasting food was a religious fault and so Our Lady was apt to be displeased if we didn't finish everything on the plate. (Josephine A. Wilson)

The nuns were the means by which we knew what the Almighty's views were on things. They spent so long in communication with Him and the saints that I suppose we took it for granted that they were more familiar with His opinions than we were. As for Our Lady, the Virgin Mary, they seemed to know what she thought about every single thing we did or might be tempted to do. They would say, 'Our Lady grieves when she sees' whatever it might be. One of the things that Our Lady couldn't abide was the sight of a girl sitting with her legs crossed. Why this should upset her so much, I could never fathom out, but they would tell us solemnly that, 'Our Lady blushes every time she sees a girl with her legs crossed.' Obviously, we suffered agonies at the thought that we were upsetting Our Lady in this way. I went to a Catholic boarding school for girls, run by the Ursulines. (Anon)

Apart from the million petty rules which I am firmly convinced had been devised to keep us under control during the daylight hours, there were even rules for when we were asleep. When I first went to school, a nun came round to see that I was settling in okay, and when she saw me sprawled in bed, she was horrified. This was not, apparently, what either Our Lady or the Lord liked to see. We should compose ourselves when we were falling asleep in such a way that if we died in the night, we would look neat and tidy. The nun actually talked to me of dying in the night. I was only eleven and it terrified me out of my wits. I thought that girls dying during the night was the sort of thing which happened all the time there! She got me to lay on my back and fold my hands in front of me, rather like a corpse which has been laid out for burial. Even at that age, I realised that there was something a bit odd about it. (Anon)

In faith schools, the staff could use the Deity both as an infallible and ever-present member of staff and also as the ultimate disciplinarian. Small children were told, 'Jesus sees what you are doing, even if nobody else is there.' The threat of hell was a very real one for naughty boys and girls under the supervision of nuns. Some nuns told awful stories about children who had died while in a state of mortal sin and would therefore have gone straight to hell once they had passed away.

I went to a Catholic primary school in the early 1950s and we heard a lot about hell. God seemed to be permanently angry with us for one thing or another. I didn't really grasp the finer points of the theology, but sins were either mortal or venial. A mortal sin meant that unless you dashed off to confession and died without repenting, then there was only one place you were headed and it definitely wasn't heaven! There was also an unforgivable sin of blaspheming against the Holy

Ghost. I worried terribly that I might have committed this sin without realising it and that meant that whatever I did in the future, I was still damned; it was the one thing that Jesus said couldn't be forgiven. I gather things are a little less like this in Catholic schools now and I dare say that that's because there are fewer nuns teaching. (Sheila Fawcett)

Today, it is very unlikely to come across a teaching nun. Teachers of this kind were to be found only in Catholic schools. Although much has been said about Catholic schools and the way in which nus taught their pupils, one thing which is indisputable is that these women were utterly dedicated to their job, and they were wholeheartedly committed to their work.

I would not say that the nuns who taught us were cruel, but nor would I describe them as kind. They were completely devoted to their vocation and teaching a lot of awful teenage girls was part of that. The majority of the teachers at our school were nuns and the head was the Reverend Mother. They taught us not only the academic stuff that we had to learn, but more important to them was our moral and spiritual life. They did not miss a trick and always seemed to know what we were going to get up to before we knew ourselves. It was more important to them that we grew up to be decent Catholic women than that we left school with a bunch of GCEs. Having said that, the academic standards of the school were very high and a lot of us went on to university, which wasn't as common in the 1950s as it is now. (Jospehine A. Wilson)

Teaching nuns had two equally important tasks, whereas most teachers had but one. The average teacher's timescale consisted of five years in the lower school, two years in the sixth form, three years at university. The nuns, on the other hand, were working from a perspective of eternity. It was of infinitely greater concern to them where their pupils would be spending eternity. Set against this, the year or two spent at university, or even few decades in a career, were really trifling affairs.

I attended both an ordinary school up to the age of eleven and then a Catholic secondary school from 1951 onwards. The emphasis on being 'good' was enormous. This did not mean just in the sense of not breaking rules or being caught out, but was more an inner quality which we were encouraged to nurture. Whatever sort of life we led in this world, whether it was a successful career or looking after a home as a wife and mother, it was all just a short prelude before eternity began. Then we would see who had been a success and who a failure! It meant little to the nuns who was getting the top marks in maths or who was in line for a place at Cambridge. What mattered far more to them was what was in the heart of a girl. This meant that the situation was quite the opposite of that in a 'normal' school. There, if you were top of the class and never got into trouble, you were the teachers' favourite. In our school though, you could do all that and still be the worst girl in the school, because you might be afflicted with the awful sin of pride, which would offset all the outward achievements. (Anon)

There are very few teaching nuns in this country today and teaching staff of this kind are very much a dying breed. In the late 1940s, though, and throughout the 1950s, it was possible to attend a school where almost all the teaching was by nuns and, as the account above suggests, their standards were hugely different from those of secular teachers in other schools.

The nuns said that I was 'bold', which was about the worst thing one could be, because it was the very antithesis of Our Lady. There was a constant looking into our hearts to see what sort of women we would grow up to be. I knew from a very young age about mortal sin and the consequences of moral laxity. It didn't just mean ruin in this world, but disaster in the next as well. Academic standards at our school were very high, but it was always made clear that this was not an end in itself. It was no good becoming a learned and brainy person if you didn't use your gifts for the glory of God. I have a lot to thank the nuns for; they taught me well enough to get me into a good university. On the other hand, I have spent a lot of my life feeling guilty about the most trivial things. I might have had a happier life with fewer qualifications and less guilt. (Sheila Fawcett)

Religion in Schools

In the late 1940s, everybody had a vaguely Christian background. Even those families who did not attend church hoped to marry in church, have their children christened and have funeral services in church for their elderly relatives when they died. It was just what one did. This use of the church for the major events of life had its foundations in the teaching received at school.

> Christianity was a background to everything we did at school. My parents weren't at all 'churchy', but I learned all the basic stories of the Bible at school. I can't imagine what it must be like today, when the children grow up not even knowing that Easter is to celebrate the resurrection. I remember swearing on a Bible to prove that I was being truthful. This was with other children and they all understood that this made the thing serious and binding. (Peter A. Barker)

The law still requires school to begin each day with an act of collective worship of a 'wholly or broadly Christian nature'. Today, this provision of the 1996 Education Act is almost completely ignored.

> Every morning before lessons, we all gathered in the hall for what was, in all but name, an Anglican Church service. We had prayers, hymns and a reading from the Bible. The only people excused from assembly were the Jews. Catholics – or RCs, as we called them – worshipped with the rest of us. There were no atheists or anybody from other faiths. (Brenda Jacobs)

I went to an all-age school; starting in the infants and eventually progressing to the secondary modern on the floor above. Each of the three floors had a big assembly hall, with the classrooms round the side. In the infants, we had prayers in the morning. We also said grace before meals; 'For what we are about to receive, may the Lord make us truly grateful. Amen.' (Harry R. Smith)

The Christian faith was absorbed at that time almost by osmosis; even by those children whose parents were completely irreligious and wouldn't have sent their children even to a Sunday school. It would be a very rare child who left school being unable to recite the Lord's Prayer.

I remember learning the Lord's Prayer in the infants. It was quite important; everybody was supposed to be able to say it in unison during prayers. Of course, I didn't really understand all of it and it wasn't until after I had left school that I even learned what the word 'hallowed' was supposed to mean. The other word I never really could make sense of was 'temptation'. When I was small, I thought that I was asking God not to lead me into Thames Station! I had no idea what this terrible place could be, but I knew that it was to be avoided. I was familiar with the local station and supposed that Thames Station was somewhere nearby that must be avoided at all costs because of the wicked activities which went on there. (James H. Schneider)

We could all name the Ten Commandments by the time we left juniors. We learned them one per week in scripture lessons. Each lesson the teacher would put a big, luridly coloured picture up at the front to illustrate the commandment which we were learning. A man making an idol for the one about not making graven images, a bank robber for 'Thou shalt not steal' and so on. When it came to the seventh commandment, the teacher did not explain it to us as she had the others, but told us to copy the picture for that week into our books. You might think that a picture designed to illustrate 'Thou shalt not commit adultery' would be hot stuff, but you would be wrong. In fact, the picture showed a villainous looking fellow pouring water from a watering can into a large container labelled 'milk'. Adultery, yes, but not I suspect the sort that the Bible had in mind! My parents were enchanted with this neat avoidance by the school of a potentially tricky problem. (Sheila Fawcett)

More children and young people in those days belonged to uniformed organisations like Scouts, Guides, Boys' Brigade and similar groups. Church youth clubs were also very popular. This was partly because there was very little for young people to do in the evenings; most homes did not have televisions and usually there was not a great deal of money to spare for outings. An evening at Scouts or a youth club was a cheap way of getting away from home for the evening. There was also the advantage with groups like the Boys' Brigade that one could go to an annual camp; a real treat when many families could not afford to go away on holiday regularly.

> The only holidays I had while I was at school were with the Boys' Brigade. We went to church most Sundays, because unless you had attended a certain number of services, you were not allowed to go to camp in the summer. This interlocked neatly with what we were doing and learning at school. Everybody was, at least nominally, Christian in those days. We prayed in the morning at school and then before school dinners and then when I went to Boys' Brigade in the evening, where there were more prayers and Bible study. (Peter A. Barker)

Youth clubs and uniformed organisations usually made it a condition of membership that young people should go to church regularly. This too acted to reinforce what was being taught in schools and to underline to growing children the tenets of the Christian faith.

In the Playground and on the Playing Field

Today, playgrounds at school are all mixed, with boys and girls playing together happily and mixing freely. This is the case in most schools from the age of five, right up to the ages of sixteen or eighteen. All state primary schools are mixed and the few remaining single-sex secondary schools are either grammar schools or in the private sector. Things were very different in the years from 1945 to 1959. Back then the idea was to keep boys and girls apart as much as was humanly possible.

We mixed together in the infants, but from the age of seven, the playgrounds were separate. In some ways, I suppose that this made sense. After all, boys' games do tend to be a bit more boisterous than girls'. From what I could make out, the boys used to charge around, shouting like maniacs at playtime and during dinnertime. It was very different in the girls' playground. The most vigorous activity there was skipping. A lot of us sat and talked or did French knitting, things like that. I wasn't sorry to have this arrangement really. Even in the infants, the boys could be pretty annoying. (Brenda Jacobs)

I remember in the infants, the headmistress, Miss Knapman, once denounced gangs and made it clear that she was determined to put a stop to them. What were these 'gangs' you ask? Some of the boys would get together and put their arms round each other's shoulders and form a line; a bit like a rugby scrum. Then they would move around the playground during playtime, chanting in unison, 'Anybody want to join the Oom Pom Pom – No girls!' The idea was to get as long a line of boys as possible, who could then sweep round the playground, disrupting everybody else's games. It was pretty harmless stuff really, but Miss Knapman really laid into this practice, saying that she knew the main offenders and that they had better stop this, or else! It is rather touching that in the mid-1950s, this was the worst behaviour that a school had to contend with. (Ronald G. Feeney)

The physical separation of boys and girls at play was enforced by the structure of the buildings and playgrounds. At some schools, the boys' playground would be on one side of the school and the girls' playground on the other. If the aim of this separation was the purely practical one of allowing the different sexes to engage in their favourite pastimes conveniently, by the time children reached secondary school the motive was plainer – to stop adolescents meeting on friendly grounds together.

The secondary school which I attended was actually two schools in one. There was the boys' secondary modern and the girls'. Both were in the same building, but we had separate playgrounds. We were totally forbidden to talk to anybody in the other playground. If you were caught doing this, it could be a serious matter. I think that the general assumption was that if a teenage girl got talking to a teenage boy, then the next thing would be illegitimate babies and ruin and disgrace. (Catherine E. Kinglsey)

Of course, boys and girls mature at very different speeds during the teenage years. Most of the boys were probably more interested at that age in playing football rather than flirting. Here is how one group of boys used to spend their lunchtimes and breaks:

At our grammar school there was a craze for playing splits on the playing field. You need knives to play this, but in those days all of us carried penknives. Two boys would face each other about three feet apart, with their legs as far apart as they could manage. Then we would take it in turns to throw the knife so that it stuck in the grass between your opponent's feet. If it didn't stick, then nothing happened. If it did though, you had to move one of your feet up to the knife. This made the gap between your feet a lot smaller. Then it was your turn.

The loser was the one who announced that the game was over. This is because once your feet started getting too close there was a risk that the knife would hit your ankle or leg. It was really just a version of chicken. (Paul M. Richardson)

The carrying of knives by boys, usually penknives, was all but universal, and aside from the odd game of 'chicken', they were generally only used for such innocuous pursuits as cutting and whittling sticks. On school days out to historical attractions, such as cathedrals, penknives were generally the most favoured type of souvenir to be purchased.

Competition on the playing field and at the annual sports day could be ferocious in the 1950s, and those who were not especially athletic remember such events with loathing.

PE was a regular, ritual humiliation for those of us boys who were not sporty and tough. Our PE master had been an army instructor and the war had only been over for three or four years. He treated us twelve-year-olds like a bunch of recruits. We were shouted at if we failed to clear the vaulting horse, belittled if we were unable to climb the ropes, and ridiculed for coming in last at the cross-country run. The whole experience of PE in the secondary school left me with an abiding hatred of anything involving physical exertion. (Keith J. Ballard)

I don't think that it would be an exaggeration to say that sports days were an annual nightmare, which I dreaded for at least a couple of months in advance. Games lessons were bad enough, but at least then it was only those in your class who witnessed your humiliation. At the sports day, all the parents and visitors could join in the fun. There was no question of not entering; this made you look sulky or like a bad sportsman; both unforgivable sins in the eyes of the PE teacher. The consequence was that I had to fail miserably to clear the bar in the high jump and make the feeblest efforts ever seen to put the shot; a horrible experience. (Glynn Mitchell)

For boys in particular, PE and games could be an ordeal. A number of PE teachers had only recently left the armed forces, and, of course, every boy knew that he would be called up for National Service after leaving school. There was often a feeling that the tougher the boys became, the better it would be for them when they found themselves spending three years in the army, navy or air force.

> Gym was not a pleasurable activity, even for those who were good at it. We were drilled, made to undertake exhausting physical activities, and then the whole thing would usually be rounded off with a run round the playing field. Those who displeased the teacher could expect to be given press-ups or sent for a set number of circuits round the field. (Paul M. Richardson)

> Our PE teacher had been an army instructor and it showed. He would bellow in fury at the weakest or slowest boys. He also had a special hatred for those who were overweight. I am sure that he used to forget that he was supposed to be doing PE with a bunch of teenage boys and thought he was back at the garrison in Colchester. On one occasion, a plump kid had fallen off a piece of equipment and Carson – that was the teacher – shouted at him, 'You fat bastard!' Just imagine a teacher saying that today; I should think the parents would be suing for compensation. (Harry R. Smith)

Girls, on the whole, had things a little easier, although sports day could also be an ordeal for them as well.

> We played hockey and lacrosse, neither of which I was much good at, but both of which I enjoyed. The mistress in charge of games took the thing pretty seriously, but most of the girls did not, except for the very sporty-minded ones. It did not affect one's popularity if you were a complete duffer at games. Sports days were something else again and I absolutely hated them. It didn't much matter if you muffed things up during a school lesson, but you really didn't want to do it in front of all the parents and perhaps even people like the Mayor. (Ellen T. Cade)

Boys and Girls

These days, the default setting for both primary and secondary schools is co-educational, with boys and girls being taught side-by-side. Nowadays, we are so used to this, that it comes as something of a shock to discover that during the years after the end of the Second World War, mixed education was pretty rare. We saw in a previous chapter that playgrounds at junior schools were segregated and quite a few primary schools were entirely single sex.

I was at a girls' junior school in the early 1950s and loved it. By the time I started there at the age of seven, I was already getting a bit fed-up with the behaviour of the boys I was at school with. The infants was mixed and even seven-year-old boys can be a real pain; going out of their way to muck up our games. I was glad to move to a school where there weren't any boys. I went on to a girls' grammar school, so I counted myself very blessed. (Josephine A. Wilson)

As a boy, I think that there was something to be said for mixed schools, although I didn't attend one after leaving the infants. The problem with boys is that they can be really awful; cruel, bullying and violent, especially when they are going through puberty. Having girls around somehow moderates their behaviour; they don't want to attract the disapproval of the girls.

In the years following the Second World War, secondary schools had a tendency to be single sex. Today, we hardly ever hear the word 'co-educational' because it is more or less taken as given that secondary schools cater for both boys and girls. It is only in some circumstances where this is not common; grammar schools are usually for either boys or girls and the same goes for boarding schools. A few faith schools for secondary pupils are also single sex, usually for girls. Secondary schools for boys alone are much rarer.

> When I was at secondary school (this was in London from 1949 to 1956) there simply weren't any mixed schools. Or if there were, I didn't see them. The grammars were single sex, but all the secondary moderns that I knew of were also single sex. Even when they shared the same building – one of those big old Victorian board schools – there would be a girls' secondary modern and a boys' one. Even the playgrounds were separate. It meant that one could go from the age of seven to fifteen, sixteen or even eighteen, without having much to do with girls at all. (Harry R. Smith)

> I went to a grammar school and we had no contact at all with boys. Once in a while, we would have a joint venture with the boys' grammar – to a play or a concert – but my God that was strictly policed to ensure that we only talked about the business in hand. There was no standing around chatting and getting to know each other. Everybody, by whom I mean parents and teachers, were terrified of any sexual activity on our part. In a way, you can understand it. This was the early 1950s and there was no such thing as the pill. Getting pregnant could still ruin a girl's life and all the adults around us did their best to see that this didn't happen. (Ellen T. Cade)

There were sound reasons, both educational and practical, for educating boys and girls separately, particularly after the age of eleven. For one thing, having members of the opposite sex around during and after puberty is likely to distract teenagers' minds from such mundane matters as trigonometry and the principle exports of South America. This is just as true today as it was in the 1940s.

> When me and my mates started going out with girls, we hadn't really talked to girls before and so there was a kind of mystery about them;

they were something new. So, for the first few dates, we would be mainly talking. It was fascinating to me to find out about girls; how they thought, what they were interested in and things like that. It was like meeting somebody from a foreign country really. This doesn't happen so much now, of course, because teenage boys and girls are being taught side-by-side in the same classroom. (Harry R. Smith)

There was a lot of excitement in meeting up with boys. We weren't allowed to have anything to do with them in theory and so they were rather strange and unknown creatures. You wondered what they thought and how they felt. It was exciting to get to know about this new species and try to figure out what made them tick. I was at a grammar school during the 1950s and I can truthfully say that up to the age of fourteen or fifteen, I had hardly exchanged half a dozen words with a boy who wasn't a relative or something. There just weren't the opportunities. (Josephine A. Wilson)

Most people would probably regard the greater familiarity of boys and girls with each other as a healthy development in the lives of school-children. It may be better for boys and girls to be taught together at school, but were there any advantages to this system that have now been lost?

One thing about having classes of just girls was that none of us ever felt embarrassed about putting our hand up and answering questions. We were happy to show how much we knew or were learning. I went to a grammar school in the early 1950s and it was the most fantastic environment for an intellectually lively teenage girl. There were no distractions from getting on academically and no stigma in doing your best. As a former teacher myself, I have seen how things have changed now and not for the better as far as girls are concerned. In mixed classes, it is the boys who show off and if a girl answers too many questions, she is the subject of silly remarks by the boys. The result is that many girls don't want to appear too bright. They are also engaged in relationships with boys at an early age, which distracts them from their schoolwork. Co-educational schools are great for boys, but for intelligent girls they are a bit of a disaster. (Ellen T. Cade)

Most secondary moderns were single sex when I took my 11-plus, which I failed. The one I went to was mixed though and I hated it. The boys didn't like girls answering in class and would mutter really unpleasant things under their breath. Clever girls were not popular with the boys. They weren't too popular with some of the other girls either, the ones who were setting the pace, as it were. I passed the 13-plus and went to an all-girls' grammar school and the difference was unbelievable. Here, you were expected to shine and nobody made any silly remarks if you did your homework and answered questions in class. It was a complete reversal; here it was the girls who didn't try hard who were looked down on a little. (Brenda Jacobs)

I don't think that we missed out on anything by not going out with boys until we had turned sixteen or seventeen. Our grammar school was a very vibrant, all-female society which fulfilled all our needs until we were in the upper sixth. I can't think that having a load of boys around would have made things better. (Dorothy Dobson)

With the free and easy mixing of teenage boys and girls we see today, it is hard to believe that well within living memory, teenagers of the opposite sex could seem more like mysterious aliens than fellow human beings! An evening spent with a girl could be a memorable experience for a boy of fifteen, because just talking at length to a girl was such a novelty. This state of affairs, which was once the rule in Britain, is now exceedingly rare; found only, perhaps, in those who attend boarding schools. For the average pupil in this country, it is impossible to imagine a world where teenagers do not mix freely and get to know one another naturally at school.

We live near a secondary school and I watch the kids going home at the end of the afternoon. You see boys walking with their arms round girls, groups of boys and girls together, everybody larking around and behaving as though being part of a mixed society of male and female teenagers is the most natural thing in the world; which, I suppose, to them it is. At my school, which admittedly was a convent school and very strict about such things. We were not even allowed to talk to boys in the street when we were in uniform. I knew girls who had been reported to the head for simply chatting to a cousin or brother at a bus stop. This was only the late 1950s. The only contact we would have with boys might be when some cheeky lad from the nearby secondary modern would call over to us from across the street. We simply didn't talk to boys in our day-to-day life. (Josephine A. Wilson)

Qualifications

Today, every pupil attending a state secondary school is expected to take examinations; usually the General Certificate of Secondary Education, known as GCSEs.

> I wouldn't have said that my grandson was very academic, but when he was sixteen he passed eleven GCSEs. When I was his age, those at the secondary moderns took no exams and even the ones at the grammar school counted themselves lucky if they passed five GCEs. Today, they come out with dozens of the things. (Lillian O. Drake)

Just to remind ourselves, before the Second World War only about 10 per cent of children at state schools gained any sort of qualification. The great majority left at fourteen with nothing at all. Between 1945 and 1951, the qualifications which children at grammar schools hoped to leave with were the School Certificate and the Higher School Certificate. These were, very roughly, equivalent to the present-day GCSEs and A Levels. The School Certificate was taken by those leaving school at sixteen and the Higher was taken by young people who stayed on in the sixth form. Being granted the School Certificate was known as matriculating.

For the first few years of the selective system, these qualifications remained unchanged. To get the School Certificate, one had to reach a certain level of proficiency in six subjects, which had to include English and mathematics. Because so few young people were passing the School Certificate, it was not the big commercial concern that qualifications have today become.

> I was at a high school and matriculated in 1947. Getting your 'matric', as we called it, wasn't very hard. In fact, I think everybody in our class got it. It was based partly upon our work and also upon test results. I don't think that it can have been too hard; there was no revising and cramming for exams the way it is now. In fact, it was just a routine thing. You went to a grammar school and at the end of the fifth form, you matriculated. All that your School Cert really showed was that you had been to a decent school and stayed there until you were sixteen or eighteen. (Mary Olive)

The School Certificate was expected to be passed and usually was. When the General Certificate of Education was introduced in 1951, it caused uproar. It was now quite possible for a child to fail his or her exams after spending five years in a grammar school; a thing which was pretty rare with the old School Certificate. When the first results came through in the spring of 1952, there was dismay among pupils, parents and teachers alike. The following account highlights that sixteen-year-olds had, like the year above them, simply taken it for granted that they would be walking out with their certificates for five or six subjects, just as had been the case with the School Certificate. They were very much mistaken.

> My parents nearly had heart failure when the results of my GCEs came through. I was the youngest of three and my brother and sister had both matriculated without any difficulty at all. Five years at the grammar school, collect your School Certificate as you left; it was pretty much as easy as that. I sat six subjects and failed three. This meant that I couldn't go on to the sixth form, which in turn meant no university for me. My parents were furious about it, but I wasn't alone. In that first year, about half of those taking the new General Certificate of Education, which had replaced the School Cert, failed. Instead of the standard six subjects, they were getting two, three or four. (Paul M. Richardson)

After the first GCE results in 1952, some teachers suggested that the examinations were too hard and that the marking should be adjusted so that practically any child could pass and leave with the same clutch of subjects, as had been the case with the School Certificate. For them it seemed to be something of a swindle that they spent years teaching these children, only to see them recieve no qualification. The format of the new GCE was virtually identical to the old School Certificate, at least in the early years. Critics of the new qualification missed the point entirely; that this was the whole purpose of the thing – the brighter sixteen-year-old would be distinguished from the less able.

> I remember my teacher being very scathing about the GCEs a year or
> so after they were brought in. This must have been in 1952 or 1953.
> He honestly couldn't see why so many of the boys he had taught
> history to were not passing the exam. The explanation is that the pass
> marks were deliberately increased for the new exams. I think that the
> pass level for the School Cert had been something ridiculously low,
> like 33 per cent, and this had been raised to 45 per cent, I think. This
> meant that those who had just coasted along, doing just enough work
> to keep out of trouble, were likely to fail. Up until then, everybody had
> assumed that the new exams wouldn't really make any difference and
> that those of us at grammar school would just be collecting our six
> subjects as before. (Conrad Summerfield)

None of this affected those at secondary moderns, as they were still leaving school at the age of fifteen. Another feature of the new GCE was that one could not sit it before the age of sixteen. This requirement was later dropped, but while it was in force, it made it completely impossible for anybody at a secondary modern to even consider taking a GCE.

The General Certificate was better in some ways and worse in others. You could leave with seven or eight subjects or one, or even none. This wasn't the way it was with the old School Certificate – if you didn't pass your six subjects, then no certificate.

> I didn't do as much work as I should have for history in the year that I
> was due to matriculate. This was just before they brought in the new
> General Certificate. I thought it would be OK, because I was brilliant
> at maths and English, also the other subjects like biology. Imagine my
> shock when I failed history and found that that meant that I couldn't
> matriculate. It didn't matter how good my maths was, the fact that

I didn't pass in all six subjects meant that I couldn't get my School Cert.(David P. Taylor)

School children can be very reactionary in many ways, being almost as opposed to change as some older people. The school cert was familiar and you knew where you were with it. Neither we nor our parents, nor I think even the teachers themselves, had any idea what was going on with the GCEs when they brought them in. We felt like guinea pigs for some cruel new experiment by the government. In retrospect I can see the nature of the problem. My parents and other relatives had scraped through the school cert and the higher, getting to university on what was really a pretty poor standard of educational achievement. It was almost as though pupils in grammar schools felt that passing the school cert was just a routine thing that you did at sixteen, followed by passing your highers at eighteen. I never heard of anybody staying on at the sixth and not passing highers. The GCEs and A levels changed all that and were real tests of ability. That's why we were nervous about them! (Conrad Summerfield)

We heard that in some secondary moderns pupils were being allowed to take GCEs and that they had been passing them as well. Such a thing never happened in our school. Without exception we left at fifteen with nothing much to show for our time at school. We had references from the school, stating that we had studied this subject or that, but that was all. (Catherine E. Kingsley)

The aim was really to get five GCEs. Today. this was what they call the benchmark. Many jobs stipulated five GCEs and you would be unlikely to get into the sixth without this bare minimum. It doesn't sound many these days, when all the kids are leaving school with a dozen GCSEs, but those GCEs were hard to pass. Instead of the different grades which you get now, it was really just a question of passing or failing. (Paul M. Richardson)

Into the Sixth

We have looked at the experience of children at different types of school, including grammars, secondary moderns, comprehensives and independent schools. It is time to look at one aspect of school life which only a tiny minority would have enjoyed during the 1950s; education beyond the age of sixteen. Of those who secured places at grammar schools, at least the possibility existed of further education, although not all took it up. Of those who remained long enough to gain any qualifications, only a small number carried on to take A Levels.

My parents insisted that I went into the sixth and took my A Levels. I didn't really want to, because all my mates were leaving. I soon noticed that in the Lower Sixth there were hardly any other boys like me. I was from what I would call an 'ordinary' home. My parents didn't have very much money and I was the first person in the family to go to a grammar school. Because of this, I didn't really have a set to hang round with in the sixth. I coped with the work well enough, but felt isolated and lonely. Everybody else's fathers seemed to be doctors and solicitors, while mine worked on the railways. I left after the first year and so didn't take A Levels in the end. (Glynn Mitchell)

The sixth was like a cut-price version of some independent school. A lot of the other girls put on very posh voices and pretended that they were somewhere quite exclusive. I was alright, my parents were fairly well-off and I had attended a private school until I was eleven, so I fitted in. There were a few girls who didn't speak in the 'right' way and were pretty well shunned. I feel ashamed to remember it now, but you know what girls can be like at that age. (Anon)

In the mid-fifties a government report was produced which examined in detail the problem of children who left school early. It was discovered that the majority of early leavers came from working-class families and it was recognised that this created an issue for what we now call 'social mobility'. Some children left school at the first opportunity because their family desperately needed another wage earner to make ends meet, but even when this was not the case, many children from poorer backgrounds felt reluctant to stay on in an atmosphere which was not really congenial to them.

We need to bear in mind that in 1950, only 5 per cent of young people were being given places at university. This figure has increased almost ten fold since then, and continues to rise. Having a child go to university today is so run-of-the-mill as to be wholly unremarkable, but in the 1950s it was a rare event indeed.

My parents just couldn't take it in when they realised that I would be going off to university. We lived in Salford and I think it fair to say that few young people in that area ended up studying medieval languages at Exeter University. Exeter! It might as well have been Tibet for the way that my parents and grandparents talked about it. It's hard to convey the mystique that university held for people of our background at that time. It symbolised everything that people like us had never before been able to aspire to. Even the neighbours were hugely impressed. I have heard other people say that neighbours in working-class districts could be a bit funny about that sort of thing and assume that one was becoming snobby and getting above one's station in life; but I never felt anything of that kind. The people next door gazed at me in awe, as though I were going off on a pilgrimage to some fabled land. Of course, not all those going to university were regarded in this light. For some, it was seen simply as the natural progression from school. (Ellen T. Cade)

In the late 1940s it was still possible for families to pull strings on university admissions. My father had been to Balliol in Oxford and he intended to make damned sure that I went there too. I don't know precisely what means he employed, but I remember his ringing up old friends and then driving up to Oxford one evening. Whatever he did, it seemed to have worked, because I got in despite some pretty poor results in my Highers. It was all just passes, rather than credits or distinctions. (James R. Harker)

Going on to university was the whole point of going into the sixth form. The Higher School Certificate or A Levels were designed to identify those who would do well at university and were suited to academic study. If one wished to get a job after school, then a decent bunch of GCEs would be more than enough for the purpose. Many employers during the 1950s specified a certain number of GCEs as a prerequisite for a job; few or none required A Levels. Banks and civil service departments would, for example, advertise posts for which five GCEs were needed. The only reason one would really take A Levels was to get to university.

All sixth forms had restrictions on entry. These usually took the form of gaining the School Certificate, perhaps with a certain number of credits, and then later gaining five GCEs. The old GCE was easily failed completely, and passing five of the things did argue for a fairly high level of achievement. Although passing those five GCEs was the basic requirement, it did not guarantee one a place in the sixth – heads had great latitude in matters such as who could and could not enter their sixth form.

I was not exactly a favourite of the head! I was on track for getting at least five GCEs, but he summoned me to his study and asked me if I wouldn't be happier in a technical college. I had actually thought of this for myself, but I was bloody-minded enough to dig in my heels and insist that I wanted to stay on and go into the sixth. I was very bolshie in those days, and I think that that was what he disliked, rather than the fact that I was from a working-class background and tended to drop my aitches. In the end, he reluctantly agreed that if I got the GCEs, I could have a place at the sixth. Having got my way, I applied that week to a local college and went there instead. (Keith J. Ballard)

I was refused a place in the sixth, on the grounds that my record of conduct suggested that I was not suitable for it and I might prove to be a disruptive influence. It didn't matter how many GCEs I passed, the head did not intend to have me in her sixth! (Josephine A. Wilson)

Life in the sixth form was supposed to be a step up from ordinary school and a kind of half-way house between school and university. Pupils were given more responsibility and expected to be able to work without the threat of punishment. In boys' grammar schools, pupils were addressed by their first names rather than, as was usual in the lower school, by their surnames. In both boys' and girls' schools, the sixth was when pupils became prefects, games captains and so on.

> When I started in the first form at the age of eleven, the prefects seemed to be impossibly remote beings, almost on the same level as the masters. The prefects took responsibility for a lot of the day-to-day discipline in the school. They were more likely to stumble across something discreditable than were the masters, who tended to stay in the masters' common room when they weren't actually teaching. Becoming a prefect myself in the sixth was a glorious feeling of power. I could order some hapless kid to do a load of lines for me or to write an essay on some hideously obscure subject which would keep him busy for a few lunchtimes in research. We had special crests on our blazer pockets and braiding on our sleeves, so that everybody could tell at once how important we were. (Conrad Summerfield)

> It is a horrible thing to admit, but I loved the authority I had as a prefect. Our school was a miniature world and prefects were about as high as one could rise in it, unless you were a teacher. We could boss younger girls around, set them 'impositions', report them to the head; our powers were dizzyingly extensive! Of course, for some of us, this power went to out heads and turned us into unpleasant little dictators. You have to remember that for years, we had been at the bottom of the heap and now we had found our way to the top. It was a little intoxicating. (Anon)

Sixth formers could usually be recognised on sight because their uniforms were slightly different from those of pupils in the rest of the school. In addition to a different outward appearance, sixth formers were granted special privileges which also marked their status as being higher than other pupils. In some schools, there were entrances which could only be used by masters and sixth formers, or gardens and quadrangles restricted to those in the sixth.

The aim of all this was to make both the sixth formers themselves, as well as younger pupils, feel that they were now different. These were young men and women who were probably destined for university, followed, presumably, by a glittering career. Many sixth formers and almost all prefects took very readily to this new social structure.

Today, there is a great deal more informality and equality between teachers and pupils. The distinction between various stages in school life is no longer as sharp as it was sixty years ago. True, being in the sixth form is still seen as a step up in status, but sixth formers are seldom given the kind of authority over younger children as was once the case.

Comics, Magazines and Books

One of the great complaints made by teachers in the years after 1945 was about the difficulty in getting children to read 'proper' books. Many children seemed to prefer comics to books and these were seen as being a most unacceptable and unsuitable substitute for real books. There were several reasons for this opposition to the reading of comics. One was that there was little actual text, and even a child who was barely literate could follow the narrative simply by looking at the pictures. It was also thought that reading material of this sort would sap a child's desire for books.

> Comics were absolutely and unconditionally banned at our school. They were confiscated and instantly destroyed. This applied equally to copies of *The Rover* and to the American 'horror comics' which some of the boys read. Reading *The Rover* would attract only contempt and summary destruction, but possession of horror comics was regarded as a serious and punishable matter. Even *Girl*, which was edited by a clergyman, was not exempt from the rules about comics. (Brenda Jacobs)

> In the secondary modern I attended, we only wanted American comics. Horror comics were the most popular, of course, but *Superman* and *Batman* comics were also collected and exchanged. Bringing horror comics to school was a caning offence. (Harry R. Smith)

These so-called 'horror' comics were another reason why teachers felt that the reading of comics was not a suitable influence upon their pupils.

The comics for the younger boys and girls, *The Beano* and *The Dandy* for example, were thought to encourage cheekiness and the use of slang. The American horror comics were believed to be far worse than this. They were blamed in part for the rising tide of juvenile delinquency which seemed to be sweeping Britain in the early 1950s.

The horror comics were a phenomenon of the 1950s, and for a time were thought to be a threat to the nation's children in the same way as gory computer games and unsuitable DVDs are viewed today. They were first brought into this country in the early 1950s and to begin with were only available in major ports such as Liverpool and London. They had titles like *Vault of Horror*, *Tales from the Crypt*, and *Sinister Tales*. These varied from lurid, full-colour comics to cheaper versions in smudgy black and white. All showed gruesome scenes of murders, executions and sexual crimes; which is, of course, precisely why boys at secondary schools were so keen on them.

Horror comics were not only banned in schools, the government acted to prevent their importation into the country at all. The fuss about horror comics turned into what has been described as a 'moral panic'. Outrage by teachers and parents eventually reached Parliament, and the Archbishop of Canterbury himself denounced them. The Home Secretary at the time, Major Gwilym Lloyd George, introduced legislation to ban horror comics, so dangerous had they become in the popular imagination.

Little wonder that horror comics became so attractive to boys at secondary schools, what with such fierce condemnation from every adult from the Archbishop of Canterbury and Home Secretary right the way down to their teachers! Nothing could be more guaranteed to make the things irresistible to the average teenage boy.

Vault of Horror was great. Some of the stories were so horrible that I could hardly sleep after reading them; people being buried alive, ghastly mutilations, graphic depictions of men being gassed and electrocuted. They were all that I read for a year or two. Even after they were made illegal, there were still plenty of them around. After the law was passed, we had to be extremely careful not to be caught with them. Our head made several speeches in assembly denouncing them and telling us that they were now against the law. He also said that he would contact the police if any boy was found with them, but I never heard of this actually happening. (Glynn Mitchell)

Horror comics! There was nothing to match them, certainly not anything being published in this country. Comics like *Eagle* or *Hotspur* might have been okay for the kids at grammar school, but for us, nothing could equal the American comics. My own favourite was *Tales from the Crypt*. (Ronald G. Feeney)

Although American comics were in demand, British comics too enjoyed very high circulations at this time. The 1950s can be regarded as the heyday of British comics. For some reason, perhaps connected with the fact that boys tend to be less keen on reading books than girls, there were far more boys' comics in the 1950s than ones for girls. *The Rover, Hotspur, Tiger* and *The Wizard* were all eagerly bought each week and then lent to others or perhaps swapped for comics that had not yet been read.

It could be said that comics were so popular at the time, because they gave an alternative view of the world to that which was found in books of the time. The attraction of comics and the disenchantment with the books found at school began very young for some children. Let us begin by looking at the first book which most children would encounter at school – Book 1 of the Janet and John series. These books were attractively produced in full colour and were certainly a great improvement on the sort of reading schemes which had gone before, but there was a bit of a problem with them. Janet and John led a life utterly remote from that of many children in state schools at that time.

These children lived in large detached or semi-detached houses with absolutely enormous gardens. Their homes were beautiful places, furnished with marvellous toys and immaculately decorated. They seemingly lived in some sort of sylvan paradise; neither town nor country. The illustrations in the book show no sign of habitation, or of farmland; in some there are bridges, which suggest that the children live and play near a river. Try for a moment to imagine what illustrations of this sort would look like to a child growing up in terraced houses in inner-city Manchester or the East End of London.

I simply couldn't get my head round Janet and John's adventures. The house they lived in looked huge and their parents apparently only had two children. The backgrounds looked like nothing I had ever seen. It was all flowers and trees, with quaint rustic seats and little stone bridges.

I grew up in a two-up, two-down in Salford. I had four brothers and sisters and my mother hardly had time to do anything with us, she was that busy. Janet and John's mother didn't actually appear to do anything at all except play with the kids and put them to bed. I simply couldn't relate to the Janet and John books! I could never make out whether they were meant to be real children or if it was supposed to be some sort of fantasy world. It certainly didn't bear any relation to anything in my life. (Ellen T. Cade)

All these books, comics and magazines could not have been intended for the comparatively small market of children from well-off backgrounds who were actually at boarding schools. Most of those who read the *Famous Five* books, for instance, must have come from far more modest homes and been attending ordinary state schools. Few could have had firsthand knowledge of the kind of families about which they were reading. Take this classic example from one of Enid Blyton's school stories – in this case, *The Twins at St Clare's*.

One of the girls at the exclusive boarding school of St Clare's is noticed to be talking in an ungrammatical manner. Sheila says at one point, 'You didn't ought to talk like that!' She is swiftly reproved by one of the other girls, who tells us bluntly that she talks, 'Like the daughter of the dustman'. The poor child is upset, as well she might be. How on earth has somebody without a thorough grounding in good English ended up at a decent school like St Clare's? A few pages later it is explained that, 'Sheila's parents were once very poor. Her mother was the daughter of our gardener.' Just how many children reading Enid Blyton's books had gardeners, I wonder?

Other school-related fiction was to be found in the 1940s and '50s on the radio, television and at the cinema. Anthony Buckridge, a former teacher, wrote a radio play about an eleven-year-old boy, Jennings, at a boarding school. This was broadcast on the radio programme *Children's Hour* in 1948. Other plays featuring Jennings and his friend, Darbyshire, soon appeared. In 1950, they were turned into a book, *Jennings Goes to School*.

The *Jennings* stories were very popular on *Children's Hour*, and once again we are left with the strange situation of hundreds of thousands of children avidly absorbing anecdotes about the life of a child whose existence could have very little in common with their own. During the 1950s, Buckridge's books were nearly as popular as Enid Blyton's, and not only with children. The prospect of reading the latest *Jennings* book to the children was for many parents a treat to be looked forward to on their own account, notwithstanding any pleasure which it might bring to their children.

> We listened to the *Jennings* stories on *Children's Hour* and when they were printed as books, my parents bought them. I still have nearly all the Jennings books and I can honestly say that they contain some of the funniest writing that I have ever read and that includes Wodehouse and Tom Sharp. My children loved them as well and so too do the grandchildren. Although they are set in a world so alien to them, the humour still comes out in the relationships between Jennings and Derbyshire and between the boys and the masters. True classics! (Conrad Summerfield)

> There has never been anything in the way of school stories to match Jennings. I read my brother's *Jennings* books and picked up a taste for them. When I first visited the home of my future husband, I saw half a dozen Jennings books in his bookshelf and I think that clinched it. A fellow Jennings fan would make the perfect husband! We still use expressions from the books in our conversations as something of a private joke. (Josephine A. Wilson)

Very few television programmes were being broadcast in the early 1950s, but one at least concerned the adventures of a boy at school. This was none other than Billy Bunter. The Edwardian era might have ended over forty years before the series began in 1952, but the audiences' reactions to the exploits of a bunch of pupils at a minor public school before the First World War were so good that each episode was broadcast twice; once at 5.40 p.m. for children and then again at 8 p.m. for their parents.

How was school life being portrayed at the cinema? Films such as *St Trinian's* comply with the unwritten rule that fictional schools should always be fee-paying, but a 1948 British film at least had a working-class schoolboy as its hero. Richard Attenborough, then twenty-five, starred in *The Guinea Pig* as the fourteen-year-old son of an East London tobacconist. He wins a scholarship to ... a boarding school! The film then shows how he adapts to this new environment, eventually winning a place at Cambridge; but only after losing that ghastly proletarian accent and learning to talk and behave like all the other boys from wealthier backgrounds.

The effect of all the portrayals of boarding schools and children from wealthy backgrounds in the books, films, radio and television of the 1940s and '50s was that upper middle-class backgrounds became the default setting for fictional children. There were two consequences of this peculiar convention. The first and most obvious is that perceptions of those years have become horribly distorted; we now have the vague idea that private education was the norm.

> When I was about twelve, I desperately wanted to go to boarding school. I had read all the *Mallory Towers* and *St Clare's* books, and their adventures seemed so much more exciting than my own dull life at the secondary modern. I began to feel cheated, as though the childhood that Enid Blyton wrote of was the real thing and I had ended up with a sub-standard version! (Catherine E. Kinglsey)

> I was a huge fan of the *Jennings* stories; at first on the wireless and then later when they were turned into books. I think part of the attraction was that they showed a kind of wish-fulfilment world – a world without parents. Most children and adolescents fall out with their parents, but this didn't happen to Jennings and Derbyshire because they never had to have anything to do with their mothers and fathers. I read some of my sister's Enid Blyton books and there was the same feeling there, that this was a world free of parents. I think that this might be part of the attraction of school stories and why they so often seem to be set in boarding schools. (Conrad Summerfield)

> I loved the *William* books, but even as a child, I was aware that they didn't really show the real world. William's mother did very little other than darn socks. She was not racing around like my own mother to prepare tea, go shopping, clean the house and so on. I sometimes used to resent the fact that my own mother did not have as much time to give me as William's had. We pick up instinctively that this is a family with money. If William is denied something, it is certainly not because his parents are unable to afford it. His parents stop his pocket money from time to time, but this is to pay for cucumber frames which he has smashed; it is not because they are hard up that week. (John B. Fleming)

> I really disliked the books that our teachers wanted us to read. The kids
> in them were all stuck up and most of them went to private schools. Read
> any *Famous Five* book and see how they treat working-class children.
> Working-class people in those Enid Blyton books are either crooks or
> good-natured simpletons who know their place. (Glynn Mitchell)

In 1949, *The Rover* introduced a character who would still be going strong
into the 1990s; moving effortlessly from one comic to another. This was
Alf Tupper, from *The Tough of the Track*. The introduction of this character
could be a major reason why boys at the time preferred reading comics to
Enid Blyton books.

Alf Tupper was a welder who lived mainly in a bleak industrial
environment of canals, railway arches and factories. At one time, he
actually lived in a railway arch workshop next to a canal. His diet seemed
to consist of little other than fish and chips washed down with cups of
tea. We know that Alf Tupper didn't attend a 'posh' school; he was an
orphan who, at the age of twelve, was packed off to an Industrial School,
reminiscent of an old approved school or Victorian workhouse. Alf was
a brilliant athlete who invariably beat the snobbish members of various
athletic clubs. He competed all over Britain and even abroad. Sometimes he
was so hard up that he couldn't even afford a pair of running shoes and so
was compelled to run barefoot. Even when some stuck-up bully trampled
his bare foot with his spiked running shoes, Alf still went on to win.

It was impossible to work out exactly where Alf Tupper was from, but
this was part of his charm. He would use Cockney expressions like, 'Ta,
mate', but at other times there was a hint of the Northerner about him.
The one thing we knew for sure about Alf was that he was working class
and as straight and true as they make them.

> Alf Tupper was my hero and role model when I was a kid. I instinc-
> tively disliked the children in library books, but when *The Rover* ran
> a serial about Alf Tupper's childhood, it almost moved me to tears. It
> is only as an adult that I have really understood the inversion which
> those comic book stories created to the values expressed in the books
> written for children. In Enid Blyton, non-standard use of English raises
> an immediate question mark about a character. Is he a villain? A Gypsy
> vagabond? Perhaps he is just someone from 'the village' who knows no
> better. In stories like *The Tough of the Track*, this convention was turned

on its head. You knew at once that when Alf and his mates spoke like ordinary people, it generally showed that they were good types. It was the ones with the posh accents who you had to keep an eye on – they were the real villains! (Harry R. Smith)

Throughout the 1940s and '50s, Enid Blyton bestrode the world of children's fiction like a colossus. The school stories, the *Famous Five*, *Secret Seven*, *Find Outers*, were read with enjoyment by almost every schoolchild in the country.

Enid Blyton's formula for success was a simple one. The central characters in all her books came from middle-class families. Many went to private boarding schools and those who didn't were at grammar schools. I don't believe that the expression 'secondary modern' appears in any of her books.

I loved all the Enid Blyton books. I used to buy them with my pocket money and had the entire set of *Famous Five*. As they were published, I bought them. The school library would not stock them, probably from snobbishness, and the ones in the local children's library were always out on loan. Besides, I wanted to be able to read and re-read them as much as I wanted. For years, I hardly read anything at all but Enid Blyton. I loved the way that her children were so sharp and superior. They even put police officers in their place, at least the junior ones. Village constables were always bumbling idiots with amusing accents, and the children like the *Find Outers* and the *Famous Five* would have to track down and catch the crooks, because the police were usually incapable of doing so. Pure wish-fulfilment; I used to daydream for hours about becoming involved in an Enid Blyton-style adventure. (Dorothy Dobson)

Our teachers simply couldn't understand why we were so keen on Enid Blyton. They wanted us to read classic children's books like *Treasure Island*, *Kidnapped*, *Lorna Doone*, *Children of the New Forest* and so on and all we wanted to do was read about the adventures of the *Secret Seven*. Looking at them now, I can see their point. The dialogue is awful, the plots are all very similar and they have a terribly restricted vocabulary. Even so, there was something addictive about them and I have to admit that I still sometimes re-read *Mallory Towers* and the *Twins at St Clare's*. (Josephine A. Wilson)

Enid Blyton has lasted to this day; go to any library or a bookshop and you are sure to find a shelf of her books. Her attraction for schoolchildren in the 1950s was due to a number of factors. We have already seen that one of these was the absence of parents in her stories. For many young people, this would be a dream come true. Then there are the fantastic adventures that seem to befall the children, none of whom ultimately come to any harm. Another of the great attractions of her books to hungry children in the post-war years was the obsessive attention to food.

> Rationing didn't end immediately after the war and if my memory serves me correctly, I was hungry continuously from the early 1940s until about 1955. Children naturally eat a lot and there simply wasn't a lot to eat at that time. The glorious thing about Enid Blyton's books is that there was no rationing in them. Children had as much to eat as they pleased, unconstrained by either financial considerations or the limitations of the ration book. (Conrad Summerfield)

Re-reading the books written by Enid Blyton really does show somebody with a fixation on food; for example, *Five on a Hike Together*, published in 1951, reveals an astonishing preoccupation with food and eating. In the first ninety pages alone, the following foodstuffs and drinks are mentioned by name; chocolate, biscuits, barley sugar, ice cream, orangeade, ginger beer, sandwiches, cheese, eggs, ham, pork, bread, blancmange, cake, milk, bacon, porridge, toast, marmalade, cream, honey, coffee, syrup, mushrooms and butter, and nor are these single references. Sandwiches are mentioned nineteen times, eggs fourteen times and the word 'bacon' occurs ten times; all this in just ninety pages! For children in the lean years of rationing which followed the end of the war, this would have been a form of gastronomic delight!

So far, none of those commenting on these stories actually went to boarding schools themselves and yet the books still exercised an almost magical fascination for them. Mention of magic reminds us that the most popular books in the United Kingdom for many years, the books credited with reinventing children's fiction in this country and bringing many reluctant readers to the habit of ploughing through long books, are of course the Harry Potter stories of J.K. Rowling. Almost inevitably, they too are set in a boarding school. That a series of books about life at a boarding school should still, in the twenty-first century, be selling so well says something about this topic. The boarding school story seems to have a timeless appeal.

In 1948, a new magazine began to be published for children. Unashamedly elitist, it was deliberately targeted at grammar school pupils. The *Collins Magazine for Boys and Girls* actually read more like a modern supplement from an upmarket Sunday newspaper. There were book reviews, short stories, articles on the maintenance of bicycles, puzzles and much more. Some idea of the readership may be gleaned from looking at the letters page:

> I am a doctor's daughter and we – mummy, daddy, Pat (my brother) and Jane (my sister) – live in Haverfordwest. We have two boats, a red and green canoe belonging to Pat and a rowing boat belonging to the family.

This child then goes on to talk of the river that runs past her back garden and sketches out a life which reminds one of *Swallows and Amazons*. In short, those reading the *Collins Magazine for Boys and Girls* were from families that were doing very nicely.

There is a common thread which continues from the earliest school stories published in this country, such as *Tom Brown's Schooldays*, carries on through *Vice Versa* and the Billy Bunter stories in *Magnet*, all the way through to *Goodbye Mr Chips* and the *Harry Potter* books – private education is shown as something to which one should aspire.

Bibliography

Addison, Paul, *No Turning Back: The Peacetime Revolutions of Post-War Britain*, Oxford, Oxford University Press, 2010

Banks, Olive, *Parity and Prestige in English Secondary Education*, London, Routledge & Keegan, 1955

Bellaby, Paul, *The Sociology of Comprehensive Schooling*, London, Methuen & Co. Ltd, 1977

Bennett, Jackie & Rosemary Forgan ed., *Convent Girls*, London, Virago Press, 1991

Colman, Andrew M., *Facts, Fallacies and Frauds in Psychology*, London, Unwin Hyman, 1987

Cunningham, Hugh, *The Invention of Childhood*, London, BBC Books, 2006

Davies, Nick, *The School Report*, London, Random House, 2000

Garnett, Mark & Richard Weight, *Modern British History*, London, Jonathon Cape, 2003

Grant, John, *Corrupted Science*, Surrey, AAPPL Press, 2007

Hennessy, Peter, *Having It So Good: Britain in the Fifties*, London, Allen Lane, 2006

—— *Never Again: Britain 1945-1951*, London, Jonathan Cape, 1992

Jackson, Brian, *Streaming: An Education System in Miniature*, London, Routeldge, 1964

Kynaston, David, *Austerity Britain: 1945-1951*, London, Bloomsbury Publishing, 2007

—— *Family Britain: 1951-1957*, London, Bloomsbury Publishing, 2009

Marshall, Arthur, *Giggling in the Shrubbery*, London, William Collins, 1985

Neil A.S., *Summerhill*, New York, Hart Publishing, 1960

Philips, Melanie, *All Must Have Prizes*, London, Little Brown and Company, 1996

Tomlinson, Sally, *Education in a Post-Welfare Society*, Maidenhead, Open University, 2005

Whitehead, Joan M. ed., *Personality and Learning*, London, Hodder & Stoughton, 1975

Wilmott, Peter, *Adolescent Boys in East London*, London, Routledge & Keegan, 1966

If you enjoyed this book, you may also be interested in ...

A 1960s East End Childhood
SIMON WEBB

This delightful compendium of memories will appeal to all who grew up in the East End during the Swinging Sixties. With chapters on games and hobbies, school and holidays, this wonderful volume is sure to jog memories for all who remember this exciting decade.

978 0 7524 7484 7

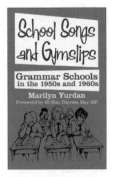

School Songs and Gymslips:
Grammar Schools in the 1950s and 1960s
MARILYN YURDAN

For anyone educated at a grammar school during their heyday in the 1950s and '60s, those days will always hold a very special place in their memory. They were the formative years of a generation. With fascinating memories and details that will resonate with thousands of grammar school pupils across the country, *School Songs and Gymslips* is a heart-warming collection of the experiences of the author and her contemporaries during a golden era.

978 0 7524 6121 2

Liverpool's Children in the 1950s
PAMELA RUSSELL

Full of the warmth and excitement of growing up in the 1950s, awakening nostalgia for times that seemed cosy and carefree with families at last enjoying peacetime, this book is packed with the experience of school days, playtime, holidays, toys, games, clubs and hobbies conjuring up the genuine atmosphere of a bygone era.

978 0 7524 5901 1

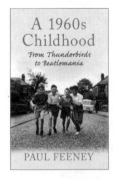

A 1960s Childhood: From Thunderbirds to Beatlemania
PAUL FEENEY

Do you remember Beatlemania? Radio Caroline? Mods and Rockers? The very first miniskirts? Then the chances are you were born in the or around 1960. With chapters on home and school life, games and hobbies, music and fashion, alongside a selection of charming illustrations, this delightful compendium of memories will appeal to all who grew up in this lively era. Take a nostalgic look at what it was like to grow up during the sixties and recapture all aspects of life back then.

978 0 7509 5012 4

Visit our website and discover thousands of other History Press books.
www.thehistorypress.co.uk